DISAPPEARED

STORIES FROM THE COAST OF NEWFOUNDLAND

Eric Colbourne

Michael Grass House

Cover design by Belinda McGee

Copyright © 2012
Eric Colbourne
Michael Grass House
Kingston, Ontario
Canada K7M 2W2

ISBN: 978-0-9879725-6-9

A tale that is not told dies.
-Old Irish proverb

This book is dedicated to my children:

Erika, Joey and Amy
who insisted I write down
the stories they were told as children

and to the memory of Uncle Eric Ledrew,
who went missing in the early 1930s

also to my brother, Maxwell Colbourne,
who passed away in 2012
and wanted to read the stories before he left us

CONTENTS

PROLOGUE

THE nineteen-fifties marked the beginning of the end for a pattern of life that had endured for a century and a half on Long Island, Newfoundland. Over the next thirty years islanders went from battery powered radio to colour television, from home medicine to the miracle of penicillin and from dirt paths to paved roads. A ferry service to the mainland closed the curtain on one hundred and fifty years of humble isolation. The story of the island is in many ways the story of rural Newfoundland.

On a map of Newfoundland, Long Island appears as a small landmass lying in the outer reaches of Notre Dame Bay on the northeast coast. Some great slumping along an ancient fault line separated the island from the mainland of the province several million years ago. Over time glaciers, wind and waves shaped it into an elfin boot with its toe stuck defiantly into the stormy north Atlantic.

The indented coastline facing west towards the mainland and northeast towards the open ocean, offers calm coves and sheltering inlets; inviting plac-

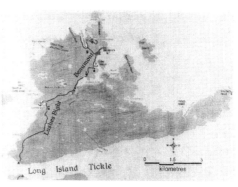

es, with the promise of gardens and grassy meadows and the lure of bounty from the sea.

Northwest from Indian Tickle is a line of smaller islands like a beaded string stretching towards the distant shore of the Baie Verte Peninsula. These rocky outcrops, some barely rising above the waves, harboured nesting water fowl. In earlier times they offered easy access to the cod grounds, the migrating salmon and the great seal herds floating by on the shifting ice floes in springtime.

From the height of land along the island's hiking trail there is a panoramic view of Notre Dame Bay and the open Atlantic. On a clear day the outline of Twillingate Island is visible, forty odd miles to the southeast. To the northeast, Cape John Gull Island, a prominent landmark, rises ominously above the fog banks.

Far to the east some 1600 nautical miles beyond the misty horizon where ocean and sky meet lies England and Ireland.

The island has always been a mystic place. The heavily forested interior of black spruce and balsam fir is dotted with spongy peat bogs and placid ponds feeding the streams rushing down to the sea. Within the deep woods there were mysterious mossy clearings with rings of giant toadstools. Islanders referred to the great mushroom circles as 'fairy rings.' On cool mornings in late summer and early fall, fog banks roll in from the ocean wrapping the valleys and marshes in mystery and silence.

Back from the ocean around the hillsides, blueberries and partridge berries grow in abundance. In the past, along the banks of small streams people harvested the fruit of the viburnum commonly referred to as squash berries. All were stored in one form or another as added insurance against the bleakness of winter.

Islanders adjusted to the harsh climate and the vagaries of weather along the northeast coast. With little more than a keen eye and an old barometer locally known as a weather glass they learned to predict weather conditions with nearly as much accuracy as today's forecasters. The Farmer's Almanac helped them divine the long term outlook, but in the end winter came early as it always did in late October and lasted until the mean days of March were spent.

They knew the ice floes borne on the southerly flow of the cold Labrador Current would blockade the island for weeks on end after the beginning of April. In some years the Arctic ice jammed the bays well into June month as though the floes were reluctant to continue the long journey to their eventual end in the warm waters off the Grand Banks. During those times fishermen climbed the high hills overlooking the bay gazing at the white expanse and worrying about the fishing season.

Close on the heels of the ice pack came the great ice islands calved from the Greenland glaciers. They floated serenely by on the tide. But to fishermen they represented danger and destruction. It was said that in every berg there existed a mean minded skipper guiding it towards the nets of unwary fishermen and into the path of schooners running blind in the fog.

After the ice had left the harbours and bays, summer crept casually by in late June and stayed for several warm and glorious months. Then people forgot about the cold, the bitter winds and the ice. Their faces turned dark with the bright sun reflecting off the sea as they pulled the bulging cod traps and tended their deep water trawls. When September came they kept anxious eyes on the southern sky and read the weather signs written in the clouds. Watching for the sun hounds, a ring around the moon or the red sky at dawn, fishermen nervously tapped their barometers. The great fall storms, hurricanes and remnants of hurricanes, were part of the pattern as well.

Stories had been handed down of the great Galveston Hurricane which tore across Newfoundland in mid-September of 1900. It caught people unprepared for its onslaught. Around the northeast coast eighty five schooners sank and over seventy fishermen lost their lives. In the island communities of Ward's Harbour and Lush's Bight boats and wharves were smashed by the heavy seas and the massive storm surge. A fully loaded cattle boat caught in the mighty storm foundered on Red Point Rock. The terrified animals were swallowed by the raging sea. Miraculously the crew survived. More than a century later the long brass anchor chain still lies stretched across the ocean floor.

The Dorset, the Little Passage people and later the Beothuk, have all left their marks here: their mamateek and storage pits hollowed out of the pebbly beaches a thousand years ago; their tool middens, where hunters and fishers pounded their hammer stones on the hard black flint and fashioned their spears and arrowheads; their cemetery, at the base of Cheyney's Head because they wanted their loved ones to be close to the sea. These sites, long since changed by the harsh climate and by curiosity seekers, are now a testament to the existence of a special people and a constant reminder of the tragedy of their disappearance.

The island was a treasured slice of the Beothuk heartland. Their annual migration down the great river of the interior of Newfoundland to their summer homes by the sea came to an end as the first West Country English began to tentatively establish a presence in the middle of the eighteenth Century. These newcomers "from the land of the bad spirit" blocked the teeming salmon rivers with their nets, built large wooden houses, laid claim to the harbours, and brought deadly diseases. The wary forest people withdrew to safer places inland. They perished there from sickness and starvation and a great silence settled over their camps.

By 1750 enterprising fishing skippers from Poole in County Dorset were making Long Island a base for their summer fishery. One of these, Matthew Ward, held rights to the teeming salmon rivers in Hall's Bay as well as fishing rights at Ward's Harbour.

The first permanent settlers from Ringwood, Poole, Sturminster Newton, and other towns and villages of the West Country of England settled at Wards Harbour around 1830. They faced an uncertain life in a strange land but hoped for a brighter future than their homeland could offer. Their strange dialect, still spoken by some island residents, was unique even by English standards. Its tone and rhythm were ideally suited to the much practiced art of storytelling.

They built places of worship in the style of the parish churches of their former homeland with lofty bell towers, vaulted ceilings and stained glass. Schools were organized. The close knit communities settled into a predictable cycle of village life based almost entirely on the unpredictable pursuit of cod. A new heartland was established.

Many villages and fishing harbours of Long Island received the names of the early visitors and permanent settlers: Quenton's Cove, Paddock's Cove, Croucher's Bight, and Cutwell Arm. In time the people of the West Country stamped a name on every nook, cranny and pinnacle around the shores of the island and on the smaller off shore islands, shoals and fishing banks; The Crow Island Sunkers, Billy Toole's Cove and Fools Cap Rock. The origin of one landmark, Doolan's Folly, is lost to history. Nonetheless, Doolan's identity and what folly he had committed remain intriguing questions.

Prune Cove has its own story. A young servant girl in the employ of a prominent merchant developed a ravenous craving for his limited store of dried prunes and one day deserted the household taking the supply of the prized delicacy with her. A search party was mounted and the runaway was located at a secluded cove feasting on the forbidden fruit and thereby provided a geographic name for the place.

AN anonymous skipper, perhaps in a foul and cold-hearted mood after a poor fishing season, left a contribution to the island's folklore by abandoning two young stowaways to their fate at a small cove in Long Tickle known since then as Milkboys' Cove. The two youngsters, former milk boys in the West Country proved their mettle by walking across the island until they spotted smoke from a settler's cabin. Here they were given shelter and taken into the family of Mr. Lush, the latter lending his name to Lush's Bight.

Most residents were no more than a couple of generations removed from the old country when the great European conflict erupted in 1914. Separation by the North Atlantic had not diminished their deep attachment to king and empire. Tiny Newfoundland, following the mother country's example, declared war on the mighty German Kaiser and the island was determined to do its duty.

The conflict, at first predicted to last several months, dragged on for four long and bloody years. Twenty-three of the island's finest voluntarily enlisted for overseas service, their names representing a cross section of the island's families; Croucher, Parsons, Burton, Caravan,

Hewlett , Rideout, Colbourne, Normore, Oake, Paddock, Perry, and Heath. Armed with little more than a steel helmet and a .303 Lee Enfield rifle, they were sent blindly into battle by commanders using the military tactics of the 1800's against the military technology of the 1900's.

Young Long Island men died in the massacre at Beaumont Hamel and in the futile advance at Monchy Le Preux; in the mud of Passchendaele and on the grassy slopes of the Keiberg Ridge in Belgium; and at the brutal battle of Cambrai. Seven of them were buried in the quiet cemeteries of Europe. Those who survived returned forever scarred by their wounds and deeply disturbed by the hell they had experienced. After the Great War the people of Cutwell Harbour and Cutwell Arm petitioned to rename their community, Beaumont, after Beaumont Hamel in honour of the young men who had made the supreme sacrifice.

The grieving families and communities also became casualties of the bitter conflict. No other event in the island's history became as seared into its collective consciousness. The proud and independent people of the island, sobered by the war experience, found renewed strength in their communities and in their culture.

The fishery was as unpredictable as ever in the 1920s and even more so in the depression years of the 1930s. Families came through the tough years with self-reliance and an abiding optimism that the future would bring a better life for their children. Schools and education were given unusual importance and in a population of nearly 800 in 1950 more than ninety per cent were literate.

By the last quarter of the twentieth century the foundation for more radical changes had been set. The residents of Long Island faced new and more powerful forces. With the decline of the fishery young people sought opportunities elsewhere and the population dropped to less than a quarter of previous levels. Those who stayed remain active in the fishery. Those who left return every summer to strengthen their roots and experience the beauty of the island's unspoiled environment.

THE GREAT PURGE

PURGE: *to purify or cleanse, especially causing evacuation of the bowels. From the Latin, Purgare, to purify. To make something clean by clearing it of everything that is bad, not wanted etc. To rid of sin, guilt or defilement. Previous word in the dictionary: Purgatory: a place or state of temporary suffering or misery.*

(The Free Dictionary)

IT WAS just before Easter, more than half a century ago, and as was the custom of the day everyone had just about finished atoning for their sins of the past year and was ready to start transgressing all over again. It was also that time of year when children in the small community were to undergo the annual ritual of purging and no one was more skillful at purging than Aunt Bess. This year she was presented with a rare opportunity to experiment with a new ingredient.

She had helped her daughter, Amelia, and her son in law, Albert, purchase a new piece of property for the relocation of their home to a site more favourable to his occupation as a fisherman. The house was duly launched across the harbour on the spring sea ice and the process of settling in began. The property had a sizable wharf, fishing shed, and a twine loft that had doubled as a prosperous retail shop run by the previous owner.

While two of the older children were rummaging

around the twine loft they discovered a large hoard of bright yellowish powder in muslin bags hidden under some loose floorboards. In their childish imagination it could only be gold and there was lots of it! After all, there were many rumours that the previous owner, a prominent merchant, was very rich and here indeed was the proof.

Their father, trying to dampen their excitement, was of the opinion that it was something that the old people mixed with cod oil to make paint. He observed that a long time ago the inside of the old Methodist church had been painted with the stuff and the resulting foul odour had caused a serious decrease in the congregation. It was part of the reason why the building had been torn down and a new one built.

The children gathered around the kitchen table watching in awe as Aunt Bess, their grandmother, took a spoonful of the golden powder, smelled it, lit a match and set it on fire. The children's eyes widened in wonder as a bluish flame rose from the spoon and a rotten egg smell filled the house. She concluded, after a long expectant silence, that the material was 'sulphurous brimstone' and her face held a curious thoughtful expression as she ruminated through the recesses of her mind for its potential uses.

Women suffering from rheumatism should use Minard's Linament. Mrs. Prathore was not able to sweep her own room, but after three applications of the linament she chased her husband half a mile with a pitchfork.

(*Twillingate Sun*, Feb. 19, 1887)

MOST people simply referred to her as Aunt Bess. It was a note of respect for a well-read elder, knowledgeable in the ways of the world, with a bent for using words that were uncommon in the little community. She referred to young men as 'bedlamer boys', after the juvenile harp seal. When someone came down with consumption and began wasting away towards death she insisted that the condition was 'Phthisis', a word which nobody else could pronounce.

Aunt Bess grew long luscious stalks of 'rhubaab' in her vegetable patch by the picket fence along with other herbs and greens that no one in the community could recognize. She lovingly cultivated monkshood, evening primrose and sage and in the bottom of her garden she encouraged a profusion of forget-me-nots, bluebells and foxglove to attract fairies in the height of summer.

She was an impressive lady, self-confident, intelligent and straight laced, a confirmed Methodist with an abiding faith in John Wesley. She had wrestled with death five times when she was raising her own children and each time she had lost an infant to the grim reaper. Everyone would have understood had she bowed to fate and become the defeated child of misfortune, but none of these tragedies had dampened her spirit nor her determination to overcome the obstacles thrown in her path.

She was a healer and when she felt the need to provide convincing evidence of her healing powers she always referred to "pod auger" days. "Back in pod auger days", she would begin. Then she would launch into a story of how this one or that one had been miraculously cured of some terrible sickness by a tried and true practice passed down from olden days when her own grandmother walked the island. "Why, one time poor Uncle Tommy Brooks had rising carbuncles on his posterior region the size of rutabagas. They were so bad he couldn't sit down. My dear granny made a bread poultice with raw cod liver oil from the stage head. Drew out the core of it in no time and the boils were gone in a fortnight."

She was familiar with the curative properties of Radways Ready Relief, Moone's Emerald Oil and Dodd's Kidney pills. She recognized that Minard's Linament could cure rheumatism and was helpful in curing baldness but suspected that C. C. Richards and Co., the manufacturer, were foreign quacks when they started claiming that it could cure diphtheria and sciatica. When they started flouting their medicine shamelessly for animal illnesses she severed all ties with the unethical drug maker.

Aunt Bess was keenly aware of medical swindlers who placed ads in the local paper promising miracle cures. She despaired at the gullibility of those in the community who were thus parted from their hard earned money. On occasion she wrote blistering missives to the fraudsters advising them, "to cease and desist on pain of legal prosecution in front of the magistrate."

She accepted that Brick's Tasteless would perk up a child's appetite but Beef Iron Wine was a plague of the devil, used by less Christian elements in the community to get drunk at Christmas time. She collected Juniper Berries and Labrador Tea at precisely the right time in late fall and steeped them to make a strong brew for treating infant colic. Mothers in labour needed Senna tea to help the baby along and as a tonic when the baby was born.

She knew the signs of Bright's disease, erysipelas, and dropsy. Senile decay puzzled her but she had a ready cure for congestion of the bowels. And when poor souls came with a blinding toothache she relied on the magic of the fairies and came up with a charm which she wrote down in a mystical language. She carefully folded the charm and hung it around the sufferer's neck.

She treated lumbago and worm fever, warts and croup. The guiding principle for her cures: 'the worse the taste, the better the medicine.'

Her daughter, Amelia, had a large and growing family of seven children in the early 1950's and was spellbound by everything her mother said. At her wits end, she battled earaches, cramps, and quincy and became her mother's willing intern knowing with certainty that she, too, needed to learn these old healing skills just in case all these new vaccines, and pills, and doctors weren't up to the job.

PARSONS' PURGATIVE PILLS Make New Rich Blood Positively cure SICK – Headaches, Biliousness, and all LIVER and BOWEL complaints, MALARIA, BLOOD-POISON and Skin Diseases (ONE PILL A DOSE). For Female Complaints these pills have no equal. "I find them a valuable cathartic and liver pill – Dr. T.M. Palmer, Monticello, Fla." "In my practice, I use no other – J. Dennison M.D., Dewitt, Iowa." Sold everywhere or sent by mail for 25 cents in stamps. Valuable information free L.S. JOHNSON and CO, BOSTON, MASS.

(*Twillingate Sun*, March 1887)

Aunt Bess was the only recognized specialist in the annual springtime ritual of purging, an event which, according to her, should take place on Easter Sunday, for symbolic reasons, but was always moved ahead to Saturday night because of more practical considerations. As she often said, "after a long hard winter the youngsters' blood is tired and full of all sorts of germs and impurities, so it's time for a resurrection."

Kerosene, a common lamp oil, was her favoured ingredient for cleansing the blood. She was aware that space scientists were experimenting with this highly combustible liquid as a clean burning rocket fuel. On one of her frequent trips to Toronto to visit relatives she had seen circus performers using it in fire breathing performances. It was therefore not unreasonable to conclude that in small quantities it could have a powerful effect on the infected blood of youngsters.

The procedure was simple even as the after effects were uncertain. A tablespoon of the dreadfully tasting lamp fuel, mixed with a similar amount of dark molasses to disguise the flavour, was forced into the mouth of each gagging and struggling child. The children were persuaded to swallow the vile blend with the subtle warning that, if not, another dose would be forthcoming.

When winters were gentle, as was rare in those days, she turned to more natural ingredients and Turpentine was favoured. She had been known to attempt manufacturing her own from the sap of the balsam fir trees which grew in great profusion behind her property. Days upon days spent collecting the sticky liquid in spring produced so little she was forced back to the commercial product.

Turpentine, as well, lent itself to many other cures besides purging. Mixed with mutton fat, it could be spread on the chest of a croupy child to ease laboured breathing and taken with a little sugar it would cure even the worst case of the worms. She had learned that even Queen Victoria favoured the product as a laxative when all other methods of inducing a bowel movement had failed. If it was good enough for Her Majesty and the Empire then no other testimony was necessary.

AND now in her grasp, Aunt Bess held another miracle ingredient! The golden sulphur found in the twine loft combined the element of fire with the natural yellow purity of the buttercups which bloomed in her garden.

She was well versed in the old beliefs and recognized that even if the stuff would not make them rich it was nevertheless a gold mine of medical possibilities. Her storehouse of knowledge indicated that the ancient Chinese had used the substance which was of volcanic origin to make gun powder and the Greeks and Romans discovered its use for making fireworks. She also remembered that it was a key ingredient in Johnson's Golden Ointment which was useful for curing catarrh, the itch, and piles. Uncle Tommy Brooks had been known to use it in modest amounts to make hens lay. Reasoning that its explosive potential and its foul odour would make it an effective internal cleanser she thus settled on a new method for purging the blood of youngsters.

On the appointed Saturday night "before the rolling away of the stone," as Aunt Bess was fond of saying, a large galvanized wash tub was brought into the centre of the kitchen and filled with warm bath water. Each child would be thoroughly scrubbed down so the cleanliness of the outside would be in balance with the purity of the inside. As the children, filled with dread and cold fear, emerged from the soothing bath, each was dressed in warm pyjamas and beckoned to come to their kindly grandmother. Amid tears and mournful whimpers, each was administered a heaping tablespoon of sulphur and molasses and sent off to bed since the purge worked best when the patient was enjoying restful sleep.

Testimonials as to the excellent results obtained by the use of PILL'S LUNG HEALER in cases of COUGHS, ASTHMA, CONSUMPTION and in fact all diseases of the chest and lungs are being received by the inventor at his laboratory in Little Bay Islands.PREPARED BY EDWIN PILL

Mr. Wm. Short of Ward's Harbour writes: Dear Mr. Pill, The effects produced by your Lung Healer are truly wonderful .A few months ago, my daughter who is 16 years old, was induced to try a bottle of your medicine for a cough attended with great weakness and pains in the chest of which she has been suffering all her life. After taking one bottle all bad symptoms disappeared and she enjoys perfect health.

(Twillingate Sun, 1884)

Aunt Bess walked home in the darkness of the April night. She reflected on the glory of the coming Easter morn with the satisfaction that once again untold numbers of germs had been slain by her medical talents and the children would remain in the peak of good health for another year.

Before turning in herself, Amelia did the rounds of each bedroom. Immediately she could detect bodily noises, like small volcanic eruptions, coming from the stomach and bowels of the children. They were restless and the smaller ones were moaning as they slept fitfully. The diarrhea began soon after and since these were the days before indoor plumbing, every chamber pot in the house was called into emergency use. One of the children dreamed his diarrhea and awakened to find the nightmare was real. By morning the laxative effects of the sulphurous brimstone had died down, leaving the children with aching bellies, and Amelia with a major clean-up job.

When Aunt Bess came by before morning service on Easter Sunday she was made aware of the severe impact on the children. However she was of the opinion that the diarrhea was a positive indication that the great purge had indeed worked better than expected. It was just that their blood contained more germs and impurities than usual this year.

In the weeks to follow, Amelia, entertaining serious doubts about the wisdom of her mother's remedies, lost interest in the store of sulphur. When several of the children came down with the mumps she convinced her husband to make the trip to the new medical clinic on the mainland.

As word spread of the great purge, demand for Aunt Bess' consulting services dwindled somewhat. It was even suggested that what came out of volcanoes should not be put into children's stomachs.

Quite by accident one day, months later, some of the children discovered to their delight that a heavy rock dropped from a certain height on a mound of sulphur would produce a decent explosion accompanied by a sheet of blue flame, and a smell of rotten eggs

I AM TAKING MY FATHER'S PLACE

Life, to be sure
Is nothing much to lose.
But young men think it is.
And we were young.

A.E Houseman, *Here Dead We Lie*

PRIVATE Heath jumped ashore on Suvla Beach in the pre-dawn hours of the 20th of September, 1915, just as the killing season was at its peak on the Gallipoli Peninsula. Along the heights inland, he could see the winking flashes of rifle fire. The faint rattle of distant machine guns broke the silence in the hills. He shivered uncontrollably as much from fear as from the cold morning air. The thousand odd men of the Newfoundland Regiment barely had time to scrape shallow trenches out of the hard clay at the foot of the near hills when the Turkish artillery spotted them at daybreak. Dolph had never experienced the terror and chaos of high explosive shells screaming around him but instinctively he hugged the ground and kept his head down.

ADOLPHUS (Dolph) Heath was born on Long island, on September 9, 1897, the second child of William Henry Heath and Susannah Sharpe. An older sister, Rhoda, seven years old at the time, doted on her new brother and the two remained close throughout his life.

The summer of 1897 had been a hot dry one, with numerous forest fires in eastern Newfoundland. The worst one, at Morton's Harbour, had spread dense smoke throughout Notre Dame Bay since July. Now, in early fall, the smoke had cleared and the harsh smell of burning fir trees disappeared as the weather turned cool and wet, giving vegetable gardens on the island a much needed boost.

Dolph Heath 1915. Photo taken at Aldershot

The bay fishery had been poor earlier in the summer and William Henry, like most fishermen had gone north to the French Shore where waters were cooler and cod traps were full. He returned in late October to see his new son for the first time.

Elsewhere in the world, the first Summer Olympics had come to a successful conclusion in Greece. Henry Ford had invented the first motorized vehicle. Powered by a four horsepower two-cycle motor, it was capable of incredible speeds of up to twenty miles per hour. Marconi had filed a patent for a system of wireless telegraphy which promised to transform communications and bring the world's people closer together. The great British Empire was celebrating the 59th year of the reign of Queen Victoria. On the horizon the 20th Century was dawning with

> I do sincerely promise and swear that I will be faithful and bear true allegiance to His Majesty, and that I will faithfully serve His Majesty in any place where I will be needed (or in the colony of Newfoundland, as the case may be), against all His enemies and opposers whatsoever, according to the condition of my service.
>
> Oath signed by Adolphus G. Heath, March 1, 1915

notes of hope and promise.

Dolph's early years spanned the end of one century and the first decade of the next. It was a time when the transition from innocent childhood to the harsh reality of adult life was abrupt. By the age of twelve, boys were expected to enter the fishery and do the same work as their fathers. At an early age girls were learning the life skills they would need to raise their own children later on.

The seal hunt and the inshore fishery occupied a man's time from April to June and then it was off to the Grey islands, the French Shore, or the Labrador until mid-October. Mothers and children cured the salt cod, tended the vegetable gardens, and cared for the sheep and goats. The men returned on the merchant's schooners in the fall with no cash but with a credit at the store to represent their meagre share of the voyage. Older fishermen were resigned to this truck system based on continuous debt. Younger ones longed to escape. It was not an easy way of life but the tiny community the Heath family called home was a safe, peaceful haven in those days. Unfortunately, death and tragedy were to be no strangers to this family.

By the fall of 1904 it was obvious that the mother, Susannah, was gravely ill. The youngest child, Josiah, had been born a year earlier and her health had continued to deteriorate since then. Tuberculosis was not a new disease on the island but one that was gaining a foothold. As winter arrived the coughing and fevers worsened and on the 27th of February, at the age of 35, she died.

Unknown to the family, William had also come down with the dreaded illness and in just over four years he, too, was dead. The historical record does not indicate whether the children stayed with relatives or continued to live in the family home at Burnt Harbour. It appears that Rhoda, now 18, shouldered the burden of caring for her brothers. Dolph was eleven years old when his father died and already had become a fisherman able to support the household. The family stayed together until the autumn of 1914 and the outbreak of the Great War.

When the mother country declared war on Germany on August 3, 1914, Dolph was still a month shy of his eighteenth birthday and the legal age for enlistment. He was a stocky young man 5' 7" and 144lbs with an adventurous streak that seems to have run through his father's family. Three of his aunts had already moved to the United States and Canada. Sister, Rhoda, left in the fall for New York where she had secured a job in a department store.

Before leaving she had arranged for Josiah to stay with an uncle and had tried unsuccessfully to discourage Dolph from joining up. With a premonition of what was to come and perhaps an appreciation of the harsh reality of war, she felt that her brother was far too young to become a soldier. Rhoda knew, however, that the proclamation from the Governor posted prominently at the store in Cutwell Harbour, and the speeches at meetings of the Long Island Patriotic Committee were creating an unstoppable enthusiasm for joining the fight. Everyone knew the war would end by Christmas and young men were eager to go before the fun was over.

Dolph notified the Justice of the Peace of his intentions and left the familiar shores of Long island in early February, 1915 to begin his great adventure into the unknown. Winter travel across Newfoundland in those days was an adventure in itself. First came the long dogteam ride up the frozen run from Lush's Bight to South Brook and then along the Hall's Bay line to the railway station at Badger. This was followed by a journey on a slow moving train taking him to the urban splendour of St. John's.

After passing the required medical exams he was assigned to No. 7 Platoon, "D" Company, 1st Battalion of the First Newfoundland Regiment on February 17, 1915. At this early stage the regiment had not fully mobilized its training facilities at Pleasantville just outside the city and the emphasis was on getting recruits overseas to the United Kingdom as quickly as possible. Training was little more than rudimentary drill and target practice with the Ross rifle.

Three weeks later the 250 men of "D" Company dressed in ill-fitting uniforms and wearing woollen balaclavas marched along King's Bridge Road and up Military Road to the Colonial Building. Prime Minister Morris addressed the troops before they continued to the waterfront and boarded the SS Stephano for the two day steam to Halifax. Dolph's companions on board ship were three other young soldiers he knew well, Andrew Pierce Caravan, Alfred Perry and Nathaniel Croucher. They were the vanguard of the twenty-three other volunteers from Long Island who would join the regiment in the next two years.

ON arrival in Halifax on March 22, the Newfoundlanders were immediately transferred to the SS Orduna, a Cunard ocean liner now transformed into a troop ship also carrying a contingent of Canadian soldiers overseas. The large ship was fast by the standards of the day, crossing the North Atlantic to the naval base at Devenport, Scotland in 8 days. The well- rested soldiers boarded trains to the old Scottish city of Edinburgh.

Their home for the next six weeks was to be Edinburgh Castle which for the first time in history would house colonial troops. Constructed in the 9th century, the imposing fortress had seen

S.S. Stephano Leaves St. John's March 20, 1915 with Dolph and the rest of D Company, First Newfoundland Regiment (Courtesy of The Rooms Provincial Archive)

its own share of bloody conflicts including its siege and capture by William of Orange in 1688. For the young soldiers from Long island marching out of Waverly Train Station and along the High Street to the ancient castle this was an imposing scene.

D Company now began a regime of basic and advanced training which would turn them into effective soldiers. They had little time to complain of their cold, brick-walled billets in the castle as a steady routine of military drill and gruelling route marches kept them busy from dawn to dusk. Only on an occasional Saturday night would they receive a short leave to sample the considerable delights of Edinburgh.

The only minor incident of rowdiness occurred on the night of the tenth of May when the Newfoundlanders were told they would be locked down pending a big move to a new base next morning. Unable to resist a challenge they simply tied their bed sheets together and scaled down the castle walls to celebrate until the wee hours in the many pubs along Prince's Street. Early next morning, amid loud expressions of disapproval from the sergeant major and many throbbing heads, the soldiers were

> **Too true it is a rotten hole,**
> **A dreary, cheerless place,**
> **And to Bonnie, Bonnie Scotland**
> **A damnable disgrace.**
> **But if I swore from morn til night**
> **The half I'd never tell**
> **And so I think I'll save my breath**
> **And simply call it Hell.**
> **...That's Stobs.**
>
> **(Joseph B. Bush, R.A.M.C.)**

ready for the next phase of their preparation for war and were moved to Stobs Camp 50 miles to the south in the rolling hills of the Scottish border country.

Despite the warm June weather and the idyllic pastoral landscape Stobs was to prove no picnic as physical and military training was elevated to ever more demanding levels. The soldiers, now housed in tents, experienced for the first time the harsh discipline of the British Army.

Their unreliable Canadian made Ross rifles were replaced by the Lee Enfield .303 with bayonet, standard issue with the British Army and considered the soldier's best friend. The young men endured punishments for the slightest infractions from chewing gum on parade to smiling in the ranks; from messy kit to public drunkenness.

Long overnight maneuvers aimed at capturing mock enemy positions gave soldiers a taste of actions to come. They practiced their trench digging skills and charged over water filled ditches to stick their razor sharp bayonets into unsuspecting straw Germans. Only a few short leaves were granted in the 12 week basic training period at Stobs. On those occasions many of the soldiers took the opportunity to travel to nearby Hawick to enjoy the hospitality of the friendly Scots.

A few engaged in lasting relationships with local Scottish girls who were to return with them to Newfoundland after the war. Many came face to face with the reality of the new kind of warfare at the front as they met the first Scottish casualties from the Battle of the Marne and the retreat from Mons with their terrifying tales of gas warfare and Hun brutality.

On August second, Dolph and his fellow soldiers, now at the peak of physical fitness, boarded trains for Aldershot for their final polishing before going to the front. The great military base just twenty miles south of Reading in Hampshire was the cradle of the British Army, the place where the country had prepared its imperial legions since the Crimean War in the 1850's. Here in the summer of 1915 more than 250,000 British and colonial soldiers honed their battle skills. After Aldershot they would be sent to the European Front or to the eastern Mediterranean where the allies were determined to capture the Gallipoli Peninsula.

The generals looked on as their enthusiastic soldiers staged mock battles featuring massed infantry assaults on fixed positions with mounted cavalry charging through the gaps to 'mop up'. It was imitation war at its best. Nevertheless, the eager young Newfoundlanders took pride in their status as fully trained soldiers and anxiously awaited their departure for the Mediterranean and a real fight with the Turks.

> **A**ldershot, August 13, 1915 Yesterday...Lord Kitchener came from London to inspect the battalion... The Newfoundland Regiment was the only one Kitchener addressed...and almost his first words were "I am sending you to the Dardenelles shortly, so be prepared, for when the order comes it will come sharply."
>
> **(The Letters of Mayo Lind)**

The record indicates that Dolph and the rest of his regiment, 1041 men and 34 officers departed Devenport for active service on the large troop ship 'Megantic' on the twentieth of August. Escorted by two heavily armed destroyers they entered the Mediterranean Sea and passed the famous British base of Gibraltar during the night of the twenty-fourth.

The great troopship squeezed into the crowded naval base at Malta the next day staying only twenty-four hours to take on extra fuel and supplies. Finally they were off on the final leg of their journey towards Mudros, the island from which the attack had been launched on the Turkish mainland, 50 miles away four months earlier. The 1st Newfoundland Regiment was to be reinforcement for the 29th Division of the British Army and for the combined force of Australian and New Zealand troops otherwise known as Anzacs.

The allied soldiers had encountered a difficult landing with heavy casualties against determined Turkish troops holding the high ground around Suvla Bay. As on the Western Front, this new theatre became a stalemate and the hillsides of Gallipoli became a vast burial ground for the dead of both sides.

The Newfoundlanders were to encounter one last delay before going into action. The 'Megantic' for unknown reasons was diverted to the Egyptian port of Alexandria where the soldiers were disembarked and sent to a military camp near Cairo.

Cairo, Eqypt, Sept., 7, 1915 You've only to look through an illustrated bible and see the sights we see every day here, the man astride his camel going over the sands, and the streams of people on asses...The people seem to be all over the place, in the shady spots from the sun...the heat is fierce, too hot for parades in the middle of the day...and during the day we have all we can do to fan the flies off us...

(The Letters of Mayo Lind)

The delay enabled the sea weary troops to wander the crowded streets of this famous capital city of historic Egypt and marvel at the sights. One of the highlights of their two-week diversion was a day trip to the Great Pyramid, the oldest of the seven wonders of the ancient world.

The regiment finally

left Alexandria on the fourteenth of September, arriving back at Mudros on the island of Lemnos four days later. On the 19th they boarded a destroyer for the final five hour run towards the rumble of heavy guns at Gallipoli. There was little conversation amongst the men and each was lost in his own thoughts.

In the early morning light the inexperienced soldiers saw the commanding heights surrounding the Suvla Plain on three sides. They were groggy and tired after a sleepless twenty four hours and a rough landing in choppy seas. Explosions shocked the men as one deadly shell after another screamed into their narrow beachhead. One exploded near a company of densely packed soldiers in a poorly constructed trench. When the barrage ended the terrified young men from the harbours and coves of Newfoundland discovered sixteen of their comrades badly wounded. For these unfortunate young men their war had ended at the moment it had begun.

By the end of September Dolph and his fellow soldiers of D Company were exposed to the deadly conditions at Gallipoli. The invasion aimed at opening the Dardanelles and capturing the great Turkish city of Constantinople had bogged down into trench warfare. A sniper's bullet or a shell burst meant instant death.

The section of the firing line occupied by the Newfoundlanders was barely fifty yards from the Turkish trenches. Back home, they would have said they were a gunshot apart. Each soldier honed his survival skills and his entire focus was on staying alive. Fleeting memories of the past, of home and family remained but thoughts of the future were erased. They existed on bully beef, hard biscuits and bad water with little variation even when the soldiers were rotated out of the forward trenches every four days for a rest. It was simple soldier's diet but not one designed for maintaining good health.

As October wore on unsanitary conditions in the trenches worsened. There was little water for drinking let alone washing and soldiers had no time to think of personal hygiene when they were under constant shell and sniper fire. A plague of lice infested their clothing. On warm days in the trenches there could be some relief by removing shirts and coats but at night as soldiers tried to rest in their blanket the misery returned. Many of the suffering soldiers came down with trench fever, a debilitating condition characterized by inflamed eyes, headaches, rash and joint pain. It was not until after the war that lice were identified as the carriers of the disease.

During the last week of October the weather on the Gallipoli Peninsula grew unbearably warm and brought with it new miseries. A plague of flies, breeding on the unburied corpses in no man's land and in open toilets in the trenches, was now visited on the soldiers. Eating became an unpleasant affair. A biscuit spread with jam was immediately covered with a black swarm before it could reach the mouth.

By October twenty-third Dolph had been feeling 'under the weather' for days. Severe headaches and extreme exhaustion had made it impossible for him to stand watch or hold on to his rifle. Now he became violently ill with uncontrollable diarrhea, vomiting and high fever. Several soldiers in his platoon had experienced similar symptoms and had died before they could be evacuated.

It was three miles from No. 7 Platoon's section of trench to the beachhead at Suvla Bay and for the sick soldiers it was the longest three miles of their lives. Under cover of darkness they were transported by boat to the hospital ship Neuralia lying some ten miles off shore and out of range of enemy artillery. Medical personnel on the ship were now being overwhelmed with the alarming numbers of fighting men disabled by disease.

Dolph was diagnosed with enteric (typhoid fever), a deadly infection caused by the salmonella typhi bacteria, highly contagious under the terrible living condition in the battle zone. The Neuralia with a full load of seriously ill Newfoundland, Australian, and British soldiers departed three weeks later for Malta. Here a large military hospital could provide better care.

Antibiotics were unknown in 1915 and it would be another 30 years before they were widely used to combat bacterial infections. Doctors treated Typhoid victims using cool water baths to bring down high temperatures along with a well-managed diet and rest to help the body fight off the infection. For one in five cases the treatment failed and the patient died.

Dolph held the advantage of having spent only a relatively short time in the trenches and with the resilience of youth was able to show marked improvement in the two weeks at Malta. When he was finally stabilized at the beginning of December, medical staff placed him aboard the larger hospital ship and he was sent to England for better medical care.

The large military hospital at Wandsworth in south west London was designated at the beginning of the war as one of the major treatment centres for allied casualties. Many Newfoundlanders owed their survival to the excellent care given by its doctors and nurses, but many would not survive their horrendous wounds and were laid to rest in the adjoining cemetery. Dolph spent the better part of December at Wandsworth before his transfer to spend another two months in the more tranquil setting of the Addington Park Convalescent Home at Croydon.

Faced with a bitter stalemate and continued high casualties the allied forces began to withdraw from the Gallipoli Peninsula at the end of 1915. By mid-December Suvla Bay was evacuated and the seriously depleted Newfoundland Regiment was assigned to assist the evacuation of allied forces further down the Turkish coast at Cape Helles. It was here on December 30th that the regiment suffered its last fatal casualty of the campaign, Pte. George Simms from Pelley's Island. George and Dolph had enlisted together.

In three months the ill- fated invasion had cost the regiment 49 fatalities while 93 were seriously wounded. Over 600 others were disabled by typhoid, dysentery and other diseases, as a result of conditions in the trenches.

IN February, 1916, Dolph rejoined his regiment at its new depot in Ayr on the west coast of Scotland where after nearly two months of retraining he was judged fit to resume life as a soldier. It was not long before the old hands along with new recruits from the island were ordered to the Western front. At the end of March it was off to battle school at Rouen, France and then a move to Englebelmer, closer to the firing line and the base camp on the Somme. The battle zone was relatively quiet during this period and the regiment rotated in and out of the trenches during April, May, and the first half of June. The situation was to change dramatically in the weeks ahead.

WILL of No. 1166, Private A. Heath   In the event of my death I give the whole of my property and effects to my brother,

Josiah Heath
Woodside Ave.
Near Rikea Ave.
Woodside,
Long Island,
New York, U.S.A.
Dated June 27th, 1916
France

Signature: Adolphus Heath

In January of 1916, Sir Douglas Haig, Commander

in Chief of the British Expeditionary Force in France, had begun the planning of a major offensive aimed at a break-through on the Somme and at pushing the enemy back into Germany. Success hinged on drenching the Germans in a baptism of fire, the likes of which the world had never seen.

Over two million high explosive shells would be lobbed into the German lines cutting their barbed wire defenses, destroying their big guns and demoralizing their troops. The 100,000 men of the Fourth Army of which the New-foundland regiment was a part would then leave their trenches in lines abreast and advance steadily across no-man's land to seize enemy positions and equipment. British artillery would lay down a "creeping barrage" fifty yards in front of their own advancing troops to ensure the enemy kept off his firing line.

The objectives for the first day were to overwhelm the three lines of heavily defended German entrenchments and advance seven miles into enemy held territory. Gen-eral Rawlinson, commanding general of the Fourth Army, voiced his concerns at the great distance the lines of ad-vancing soldiers would have to cover before engaging the enemy. His doubts were dismissed in the overall plan.

On the 24th of June, 1400 heavy guns of the British ar-tillery batteries opened the Somme offensive with a bar-rage of such intensity it could be heard 300 miles away in the south of England. The impressive display of firepower continued for the next six days and most commanders were confident the massive barrage had done the trick. At night, however, raiding parties of the Newfoundland Regiment returned from scouting missions with troubling information that the barrage was not clearing the dense barbed wire entanglements in front of the German po-sitions. Equally alarming were indications that enemy work parties were repairing at night the damage that had been done to their deep defensive positions during the day.

The battle plans were not altered to take these factors into account: the 29th Division would jump off as scheduled with the 86th and 87th brigades storming and capturing the first two lines of enemy trenches. The Newfoundland Regiment and its three sister battalions of the 88th brigade would follow, pass through their lines and capture the third line of trenches.

Immediately in front of the Newfoundlanders was the heavily fortified German position of Hawthorne Ridge. For several weeks engineers had been tunnelling deep into No Man's Land to plant

Newfoundland Trenches at Beaumont Hamel (photo Courtesy Amy Colbourne)

a massive explosive charge deep underneath the enemy's big gun emplacements. The charge was timed to explode 10 minutes before zero hour.

The allied advance was initially set for June 30th but four days of heavy rain forced a delay. Zero hour for the great "July Drive" was set for 7:30 a.m. the next morning, Saturday, July 1, 1916.

As the young Newfoundlanders crouched in their trenches they were easily identified as part of the 29th Division by the triangular piece of tin metal stitched into the back of their tunics between the shoulder blades. It was a way to identify their positions from the air as they moved forward deep into enemy territory. The twenty-six officers leading the troops held their swagger sticks in hand and wore pistols on their belts. In addition to his rifle, each soldier carried a 66 lb. pack with all the food and equipment to sustain him for several days in the field. Many soldiers were also expected to carry ladders, extra machine gun ammunition, picks and shovels. Weighed down by their equipment, Dolph and his fellow soldiers quietly awaited the order to advance on this fateful July morning.

The explosive charge under Hawthorne Ridge detonated at precisely 7:20 a.m. sending a massive cloud of smoke, rock, and other debris high into the air over the Beaumont-Hamel front. There was a ten minute silence along the allied lines and then the sound of whistles and the roar of thousands of voices as the first waves of British and Allied soldiers jumped off.

At the same time murderous machine gun fire opened up from the German positions and exploding artillery shells fell amongst the masses of advancing soldiers. The British had planned to lay down a constant stream of artillery fire just ahead of their advancing troops in a "creeping barrage".

We had eight hundred yards to charge. That was a sad hour but when we heard the word we went like lions for the Germans, the bullets flying like drops of rain and we fell like flies. We went til the last man fell. As far as the eye could see nothing but dead and dying and could see the wounded crawling for the shell holes.

I had twenty bombs on my back. I got the bullet through my knee before I got half way over and I got tangled up in barbed wire. I don't know how I got clear without getting another hit. I crawled down in a shell hole and got back to our lines alright...

(Excerpt from a soldier's letter published in *The Twillingate Sun*, August 5, 1916)

The barrage, aimed at keeping enemy heads down, did not happen. For an hour and 45 minutes the Newfoundlanders listened to the continuous rattle of machine guns, the screams of the wounded, and the thunder of artillery. They were told to get ready, then to stand down, then to man the parapet, and finally at exactly 9:15 a.m. the command to go over the top.

The bright morning sun blinded them as they jumped out of the trenches. They then began the fateful charge through the lanes they had cut in their own barbed wire. The German gunners had spotted the openings and trained their heavy weapons on the gaps. The result was a slaughter as thousands of bullets tore into the Newfoundland soldiers bunching up in the wire.

Those who did make it to No Man's Land were torn apart by shrapnel and faced a withering hail of fire. A few made it to the enemy lines only to face dense entanglements of German barbed wire. There was no way forward and no way back. The slaughter lasted thirty minutes. Every minute twenty-five young men of the 1st Newfoundland Regiment fell dead or wounded.

July 1st, 1916 turned into a hot, sunny day on the killing fields of the Somme. On the small stretch of grassy meadowland near Beaumont-Hamel two hundred thirty-three Newfoundlanders were killed outright, another 91 were missing, and 386 lay wounded in the green field. Of the 26 officers who went forward, all became casualties, with their swagger sticks and revolvers they were easy targets for German snipers. For the wounded lying on the open ground the reflective tin triangle sewn into the back of their tunic betrayed their positions.

As night fell the grim task of recovering the wounded and burying the dead began. These missions were dangerous and were largely left unfinished. Over the next five days the survivors, pinned down in No Man's Land straggled back to their lines. Albert Perry, with a gunshot wound in the leg, struggled back to Newfoundland lines after darkness fell. Nathaniel Croucher lay dead in No Man's Land. Dolph answered roll call on July 4th, one of the last to crawl back to the trenches.

It was a similar story of death and carnage all along the three and a half mile front. The first day of the Battle of the Somme had cost the British Expeditionary Force nearly 60,000 casualties. Nearly 20,000 young men died in the first twenty-four hours. The bloodbath continued until the third week in November.

THE shattered Newfoundland Regiment spent the next three months recovering. Barely two hundred fifty fighting men were left after Beaumont Hamel but new drafts from the training depot in Scotland were bringing the battalion back up to strength. By mid-September fresh soldiers, along with those who had recovered from their wounds, brought the battalion levels to over 800 men, not at full strength, but sufficient to take their place in the firing line.

Cold wet fall weather had now set in and all along the front, roads and churned up fields were turning into a sea of mud. Despite the conditions, General Haig, still hopeful, pinned his hopes on a breakthrough only a few miles to the southeast of Beaumont-Hamel. The Newfoundlanders were then given the task of capturing the German trenches in front of the shattered village of Gueudecourt.

Shortly after 2 p.m. in the afternoon of October 12th , the regiment jumped off behind a barrage of supporting artillery. This time the big British guns were successful in forcing the enemy to lie low. Aside from a number of casualties from 'friendly fire' the Newfoundlanders were successful in capturing their first objective, Hilt Trench, in a bitter hand to hand fight and continued on to the German second line of trenches. This further advance was blocked by heavy machine gun fire and taking heavy casualties they were forced to retreat to Hilt Trench.

During this part of the battle Dolph was seriously wounded, his upper left thigh shattered by machine gun fire. He was carried back to the jumping off trench by fellow soldiers and received first aid treatment from the regimental medics. Under cover of darkness stretcher bearers slogged through deep mud, moving Dolph two miles further behind the lines to an advanced dressing station.

It was a scene of chaos as overwhelmed medical staff struggled to cope with the mounting casualties from the Newfoundland Regiment and from their sister regiment, The 1st Essex which had been operating on their left during the fierce fighting. With roads in terrible condition from heavy rains another day would pass before the seriously wounded soldier would be evacuated to the 38th Casualty Clearing Station at Heilly, some ten miles in the rear.

Near dusk on the 12th, the Newfoundlanders fought off a heavy German counterattack and this time their machine guns took a heavy toll of the charging enemy. They strengthened their hard won position and looked to the wounded and the dead. The capture of Hilt Trench marked the furthest point forward for any allied unit during the Battle of the Somme. The small victory had come at an enormous price in blood. Newfoundland suffered two hundred thirty-nine casualties of which one hundred twenty were killed outright or died later of wounds.

Some forty hours later Dolph reached the 38th Casualty Clearing Station after a jolting ride through mud and shell pocked roads. He was now in deep shock and the large, jagged wound was bleeding freely. Classed as a priority for immediate treatment, doctors began the task of stabilizing the young soldier. The wound, already showing signs of infection, was thoroughly cleaned and bone fragment removed but the ever present danger of blood poisoning and gangrene meant immediate evacuation to Wandsworth Hospital in London.

Dolph had now returned to Wandsworth, ten months after his earlier stay for Typhoid Fever. The hospital was overflowing with casualties from all over the empire. It was now designated as the primary care centre for Newfoundland's wounded but was also home to the maimed from Australia and New Zealand, dominions that had also endured terrible casualties in the conflict so far.

The nurses and doctors of Wandsworth were the best in the Royal Army Medical Corps (RAMC). The operating theaters were kept busy day and night dealing with the victims of shell bursts and gas attacks, and the dreadful wounds inflicted by bayonets and machine gun bullets. Legs and arms were amputated to save the body's core; mangled intestines were cut and rejoined; disfigured faces became more disfigured with surgery and stiches. Through it all the nursing staff provided the touch of kindness and tender care that would bring the recovering wounded back from the edge of insanity and despair.

Almost immediately Capt. G.C. Hall, a resident doctor of the RAMC, recognized the gravity of Dolph's condition. The knee joint itself was showing a heavy discharge of pus, the patient was feverish and showing other signs of a major infection. Chronic pain was only eased by regular injections of morphine. A new round of surgery was ordered.

The pieces of his shattered leg bone were plated, the wound examined minutely to remove any foreign material. The knee joint was drained and cleaned. Dolph's condition was again stabilized and he appeared to make slow improvement over the next six weeks.

Despite his constant severe pain he remained in high spirits and became an inspiration for his ward mates from Australia and New Zealand. These were fellow soldiers who had come together in Egypt. They had shared the hell of Gallipoli and were again united in a great struggle, this time to overcome terrible injuries.

Christmas came and the spirits of all the wounded were lifted by nurses decorating the wards for the festive season and by the carol singing of visitors from the Newfoundland War Contingent Association in London. Visitors from the Association brought gifts of tobacco and chocolates as well as news from home. They also wrote letters to families of the wounded including Rhoda, and Josiah, in New York who were increasingly anxious for their wounded brother.

New Year's Eve, 1917 rang in with the singing of Auld Lang Syne to the hearty cheers of the medical staff and the wounded at Wandsworth. Over the next months there was little change in Dolph's condition as the stubborn infection resisted the best efforts of his doctors, and his leg wound refused to heal. He remained cheerful throughout and made no complaints about his suffering.

Easter came and went and with it the news of another great allied push on the Western Front. The First Newfoundland Regiment, still in the thick of battle, had again suffered heavy losses in a futile and poorly planned engagement at Monchy Le Preux.

By April 20th Capt. Hall knew that Dolph was in a losing battle with infection. He was rapidly losing weight and the onset of gangrene had created unseen complications. Medical staff could not reduce the high fever and his heavily swollen bronchial glands presented another complication. Blood poisoning was now coursing out of control through his body causing internal organs to shut down. It was impossible to save him. He died on April 22, 1917.

He had spent two years and sixty-seven days in the service of his country.

At 2 p.m., Tuesday, April 24, Sgt. W. C. Smith representing the First Newfoundland Regiment reported to Wandsworth Hospital to take charge of the funeral ceremony which was to be conducted with full military honours. The coffin, draped with the Newfoundland flag, and covered with many wreaths and crosses sent by the nursing staff and by the wounded Australian and New Zealand soldiers of his ward, was then placed on a gun carriage drawn by four horses with mounted drivers. The military escort, with arms reversed, was from the 111th Territorial Rifle Battalion, Wimbledon.

After a simple ceremony at the Wesleyan Chapel and a burial service at the gravesite three volleys were fired and a bugle sounded the Last Post. The weather was mild and sunny, exactly what one would expect of springtime in England. Back home on Long Island, Newfoundland, ice floes blockaded the coast and at this time of year Dolph would have been preparing for the summer cod fishery.

In New York, Rhoda mourned her brother's death. She was asked to forward an inscription for the Cemetery Registers at Wandsworth. She requested that it be a simple statement

Some Australians, New Zealanders and Newfoundlanders, who had been ward mates of the late Pte. Heath, gathered at the grave to pay their last respects. Three came on crutches, others had their heads or arms bandaged. They spoke of the qualities which had endeared the Newfoundland soldier to them all...

(from the report of Sgt. W.C. Smith

which summed up her young brother's life, "I am taking my father's place". These were his words when she asked him why he was enlisting so soon.

In her final letter to the Royal Newfoundland Regiment written in 1920 after she received a copy of the memorial scroll, she expressed her appreciation for the kindness shown to her and Josiah after the death of their brother: "I shall have the scroll framed and keep it in remembrance of my dear brother who gave his life like so many of our brave boys. I shall always miss him for I loved him very much."

Dolph's Grave at Wandsworth Cemetery, London, England (Photo Courtesy of the Beatrix Potter School)

Adolphus Garrett Heath was buried on a gentle slope in London, England facing west towards his homeland. After the war he was awarded the Victory Medal, the British War Medal, and the 1914-1915 Star in recognition of his bravery. The medals were forwarded to Rhoda.

THE BLACK ARTS BOOK

Then away out in the woods I heard that kind of sound
That a ghost makes when it wants to tell about something,
That's on its mind, and can't make itself understood,
And so can't rest easy in its grave,
And has to go about every night grieving

MARK TWAIN

THEY were children then. Now they were at that advanced age where memories from yesterday faded quickly while those from the distant past were recalled with clarity. That was how between them they could piece together a picture of what really happened a long time ago on the Island.

In those days the two children lived in a small house with their mother and father by the big brook that rushed furiously from the upland ponds every spring as the snows melted, the dark forest awakened, and the fairies emerged from their secret places. It was a time when they pulled the blankets over their heads at night so they wouldn't have to see the spirits wandering around the bedrooms nosing through the closets and flitting busily across the ceilings.

In the long spring days the children played along the banks of the rushing stream watching as small islands of foam lapped the banks before continuing on the journey to the sea. They released their toy boats into the water, sending them to faraway places like Port of Spain and Zanzibar for cargoes of sugar cane and bananas, then hurried down to the beach to watch their sailing ships tumble over the waterfall, catching them before they floated away into the busy harbour.

Just across the harbour an old abandoned house squatted mysteriously on the headland. It might just as well have been across the bay or even across the ocean because in their child eyes it was a great distance. They were raised on frightful stories about the place from their mother and her two friends, Aunt Vi from next door, and Aunt Mavis who lived down over the hill. The three women talked about many things, of course, as they whiled away lazy afternoons with their gossip. They exchanged stories about the spirits that prowled at night, the fairies that ruled the marshes, and about old Meriam, the custodian of the Black Arts Book, who used to live in the old abandoned house.

Everybody in the community knew that old Meriam had been a witch and with good reason. She had lived alone in the old house. Her children abandoned her and fled the home at the first opportunity, moving away to the mainland never to return. Her sea faring husband had died in some far off land across the seas. People on the Island said that she had even foretold her husband's death before he sailed away. His token, they said, returned as a tiny ball of light that circled the harbour before disappearing over the southern hills to take its place with the other spirits on the island.

Her very appearance cast suspicion on her character. She had bushy eyebrows that met above the bridge of a prominent nose and squinty eyes that made people feel uncomfortable in her presence. On the rare occasions when people saw her mingling in the community she walked with a peculiar bent, stopping often to lean on her knobby cane and then moving forward with her upper body almost parallel to the ground. Often, wary villagers encountered her on the forest trails pushing her wobbly wheel barrow and mumbling to herself as she collected juniper shrubs, empty bird's nests, and poison-berry bushes. At other times she sat in a rocking chair on her rickety deck facing the harbour, swaying slowly back and forth, with her black cat sneering into the sunset at her feet as they waited impatiently for darkness. There was no doubt.

Of course, all of this happened before the government came with their big machines tearing up the earth, upsetting the spirit world, and building a blacktop road across the Island so that people could lead faster lives. It was even before the time that the spirits were encouraged by whispers that came to them on the night wind that the people who lived in all the houses were leaving to resettle on the mainland. Some of the ghostly beings, in celebration, put on white coats and went dancing about on the old tracks connecting the villages. Sometimes, late at night they bumped into carousing young people from the earthly dimension who ran from them in terror.

All the spirits ever wanted, according to the children's mother, was to be left in peace to roam in the moonlight over the lovely hills behind the quiet harbours and along the gentle slopes rising from the ocean, feeding on the chocolate plums and squash berries as they drifted along, sighing and moaning softly into the warm night air

The children's grandmother was on good terms with the fairies and often left freshly churned butter for them outside her door at night. In return they rewarded her with second sight and special healing powers, although in her words, this was a mixed blessing because while she was pleased with the powers of healing, second sight was more a curse than a blessing because it forced her to witness, in real life, the tragedies that she had already endured in her visions.

She was not as well acquainted with the spirits but maintained that the fairies met once a year before the first frost with all the beings from the other world, in a small meadow, just above Joe's Hole. Years ago an unfortunate woodcutter and his pony, returning from a hard day's work in the forest, had broken through the thin ice of the Hole and had been swallowed up by the gluey mud. One clear fall night, when the harvest moon was at its brightest, their grandmother had seen the woodsman as she was returning late from another secret encounter with the fairies. The ghostly figure was covered with long marsh grass and pond lilies, as he led his horse around the bog looking for a safe place to cross.

The gatherings at Joe's Hole, according to their grandmother, were more peaceful affairs now that they didn't have to listen to the arrogant old witch who shambled in every year with her nasty imps, pushing her wobbly wheel barrow and acting like she was queen of the island. The spirits still arrived as usual with long faces, groaning and complaining about yet another meeting, their misty arms and legs hanging down to the ground. Some bats flew by, spying for the old hags that lived by Darty Pond and were too crabby to come to the gathering. A few ravens nodded sleepily in the treetops and the screech owl came by to hoot mysteriously as if he knew things nobody else did. The fairies and the spirits ignored him and eventually he grew bored with the whole thing and went back to hunting rabbits.

"Why the long faces?" asked the fairy king, sitting on his red toadstool trying to lift everyone's spirits. They all knew the fairy king was about to make his usual speech about not mixing with people from the other side and announcing new ways to bewitch children if they didn't behave properly in the forest.

"The hags are where they belong, the witch is dead and her old house is falling down," concluded the fairy king as he asked everyone present to join in the festivities before the long winter sleep.

Old Meriam was indeed dead but no one seemed to know how she had died or where she was buried, all of which added to the mystery of her life and the power of her witchcraft. After her death, the old house seemed lonely more than anything else, sitting way out on the point by the landwash, facing the September storms and enduring the sad soundings of the ocean swells. With each passing season it added a deeper tone of grey as the harsh weather of late fall and winter took its toll. Nobody in the village could understand how the old house could withstand so much punishment.

One spring morning many years after the house was deserted the children's grandmother noticed a curious bird shaped hole in an upstairs window as if some flying creature had been lured through the glass pane. She concluded, without any hesitation, that one of Old Meriam's imps, unaware that the witch was dead, had returned to receive a new list of evil instructions. Their grandmother communicated as much to everyone in town and there was renewed speculation about more misfortunes in the near future.

In fact they did not have long to wait. A young couple who found themselves facing unexpected circumstances decided to move their marriage ceremony ahead by several months. There was the usual joyous celebration in the village. Late on the wedding night word spread that Titus, the shopkeeper, and best man at the ceremony, was missing after leaving the event around midnight to walk home. Several hours later a search party of four young men found the unfortunate man in a watery ditch, bewitched and insensitive.

In his confused and frigid state Titus attempted to communicate with his rescuers in a strange tongue and tried to indicate by sign language what they should do. The young men placed the man gently into a hand cart and wheeled him in his delirium to his home where they propped him in a corner by the warm stove and placed a copy of the Old Testament in his hands. By next morning the spell had been broken but everyone in the community knew that witchcraft was responsible.

This strange incident happened just before Good Friday. It was a time of year when everyone could safely discuss witchcraft and other strange events on the Island. Aunt Vi and Aunt Mavis came by for tea and casual conversation, their faces bursting with pent up news. The two children sat quietly, listening and dangling their legs over the couch.

"That poor girl's going to have a baby," whispered Aunt Mavis.

"It's due in a month. That's what they say," added Aunt Vi.

"Shh," whispered their mother. "The youngsters will hear."

The occasion settled in the children's memory forever because their mother had bigger things on her mind. She eased into her rocking chair and announced that the family would move, lock, stock, and barrel, across the harbour the very next week. Their little home would be hauled over the sea ice right next to Old Meriam's house because it was a choice location in the community.

The announcement caused some dismay not just because of the position next door to the old abandoned house but also because in a community where gossip spread like wildfire everyone had missed the story of the pending move.

"I wouldn't be able to sleep in a house over there," said Aunt Vi, "There was just too many bad things went on in that place out on the point. That Old Meriam was the devil herself, she was."

"Well, we shouldn't be dredging up the past," maintained their mother, "She's been dead now for thirty odd years and the dead don't hurt nobody. They just become poor wandering souls, that's all..." she sighed.

Aunt Vi ignored the remark and plunged into her story.

"She had something to do with that schooner that went down, years ago, on the way back from St. John's," she added enthusiastically. "Just before Christmas it was and seven young men were gone as quick as that. Not a trace was ever found. She placed a curse on the merchant – sure, she did. He was only a passenger on board – just because he wouldn't give her credit. You'll die in a watery grave, she told him. Yes, that's what she said, You'll die in a watery grave."

Aunt Vi was encouraged to continue.

"Both of them, just like two roosters, kept up the fight outside his store, right on the road in front of a crowd of people. He called down the heavens on her head but it made no difference. She waited for her chance and when the schooner was on its way back from St. John's, she took her old black cat and threw it, hissing and spitting, into the harbour. That stirred up a hurricane of wind and the schooner disappeared without a trace. I was only a child, mind you, but I remember it like yesterday. That was some awful sad Christmas around here."

"But they came back to haunt her," added their mother, now eager to add a story of her own. "One night in late December, Jossy saw that schooner sail right in the harbour and land at her wharf. He watched as seven men, souwesters on their heads, and their oilskins dripping kelp and salt water, floated on the air right up to her door and went in. Jossy ran around shore to tell the skipper he'd landed at the wrong wharf but when he got there the schooner had disappeared. They say she went insane and killed herself after that. Yes..."

"There was another time," said their mother, "When that schooner left Jossy's wharf on a clear moonlight night in the fall and sailed right into the run, past Oil Island and past Sunday Cove Island Point, right up the middle of Halls Bay to South Brook. A man saw her land to the wharf there and went over to help tie her up but the ship disappeared right in front of his eyes. Imagine that now."

"And mind you," interrupted Aunt Mavis, "It was only a few years ago, I believe that was in December too. Anyway it was a cold night. Somebody was walking by in the snow when they saw a light in the window and there was old Miriam sitting down at her table reading her Black Arts Book, like you would. She seemed to be reading a page, and then she would get up and put things into a bowl like she was making a Christmas cake. The house went dark after a while and a strange ball of light came up from the chimney and flew off into the night sky. That book is still there in that house, you know, and God help the one that finds it."

"They say she could tell your future just by looking at your face," said Aunt Vi. "Once she met poor old Androcles Perry on the road to Cutwell Arm. He was just up looking for a few blueberries, that's all. After they were talking for a few minutes she told him he should prepare to meet his maker because he would be dead in a week. Yes, that's what she said, 'prepare to meet your maker!' Anyway, he spent the next six days going around door to door saying goodbye to everybody. He walked from one end of the island to the other telling people he was going to die. And do you know what – on the seventh day he dropped dead with a heart attack. Yes…and not a word of a lie."

"She wasn't all bad… she had cures too," suggested their mother. "But you had to be a brave soul to ask for her help. Uncle Andrew, now, had no fear of man nor beast so he went and asked her to cure his warts. He had them all over his hands and one big one on his forehead."

"Yes," she said "I'll cure your warts but only if you give them to that old scoundrel, Al Drew, down there in Seal Cove."

"So she gave Uncle Andrew a white rock, told him to rub it on the warts and put it in a place where old Al Drew would find it. Sure enough, Uncle Andrew went down to the poor man's house and put that white rock right in his favourite chair when he wasn't looking. The very next day Uncle Andrew's warts were gone but poor old Al Drew had them all over his hands and a big one right there in the middle of his forehead. Everything like that was in her Black Arts Book…oh yes."

"But she was a dirty streel," added Aunt Mavis. "Her house was a pigsty, with all that stuff she brought home in her wheelbarrow. All those cats were the worst with their scent all over the place and she never had a clothes-line."

Looking back after all those years, the two children could never remember a beginning or an ending to the stories. The women added little details here and there as time went by, like three artists working on the same painting, until eventually a complete picture emerged.

THE two children slept restlessly that night and throughout the Easter weekend before the launching of their house. They kept their heads covered more than usual at night because now the busybody spirits were joined by noisy imps and black cats with glowing yellow eyes. They awoke each morning feeling tired, yet relieved at the sunlight flowing in the windows.

The great journey across the harbour started smoothly enough on Easter Monday. The children were bundled off to their grandmother's house until the ordeal was over. Their home was fixed on skids and a large group of men came to haul on the block and tackle ropes. It moved gently down the slope over the snow cover towards the harbour ice. Once the house reached the beach, however, it seemed to suddenly realize where it was going and became stubbornly mired in the soft ice along the shoreline. It was only with the help of a draft horse and three smaller ponies that the building reluctantly resumed its journey, crossing the harbour and planting itself next door to Old Meriam's place.

After several months things were more or less back to normal except for minor creaks and moans as the transplanted home settled down in its new location and the wind found new cracks in the window sills that had been twisted and strained on the journey across the harbour.

The two children explored their new surroundings; expanding their horizons day by day until one evening after school they found themselves at the very edge of the property where the old abandoned house stood as silent and forlorn as when they had first seen it from across the harbour. The outline of a low picket fence still embraced the house but the gate had long since rusted off its hinges and lay on the ground partly covered in dry grass.

The deck, where long ago, Old Meriam had spent so many evenings in her rocking chair, had now collapsed into a pile of decaying timbers. Shutters had fallen from the windows facing the sea but were still clinging to the other windows on the sheltered side of the house. Currant and gooseberry bushes were budding profusely in a corner of the small garden.

The main door of the house still had patches of bright green paint and seemed to be slightly ajar as if inviting people inside. The two children did not go in, of course, because fear of the unknown was more powerful than their curiosity. They retreated that day but were drawn back again a week later by an uncontrollable desire to understand the story the house wanted to tell.

Even all those years later, they could remember that it was a Saturday morning in early June with a dense fog over the harbour and a silence covering the community that was broken only by the eerie call of a loon somewhere in the marshes. As they walked nervously towards the old abandoned house yellow warblers and spring robins flitted along through the mist in front of them.

They pushed gently on the green door and it swung open. The old abandoned house was silent. The two children moved as one down the narrow hallway, tripping over each other as they entered the front parlour. Other than the dampness, everything was as it must have been thirty years previously. The rain had seeped through the broken shingles on the roof, soaking several books on a small end table and forming pools on the floor. A powerful smell of mildew and decay filled the neatly furnished room. Fine china, covered in dust and mouse droppings, was neatly arranged in a cupboard. An old black and white portrait of a bearded sea captain, his cap at a rakish angle, dominated the side wall.

The stairway presented the dilemma of who would go up the steps first but after much hesitation they both moved furtively in slow motion to the upstairs landing. The doors of three bedrooms were open, and hung at odd angles. Beds had been made and a layer of dust covered the blankets. Flowered chamber pots sat on the floor.

In the small bedroom they discovered a child's bed with a rocking horse beside it covered in old cobwebs. On the dresser a small pale boy in a sailor suit peered from a water stained photograph. He was standing on the wharf besides a schooner. Underneath in a neat hand printed script, some words, now almost erased, *"John Char..., Tak... by the Sea, August 192.."*

Across the hall, in what was obviously a young girl's bedroom, patches of bright Red Riding Hood wallpaper were still in evidence. On the dresser, a young girl, perhaps ten years old, in a summer dress, smiled from a fading picture with a similar inscription, *"Annabel, Taken ... Sea, July, 19..."* There was a jagged hole in the window pane and the skeleton of a bird on the floor near the bed.

The two children left the house as quietly as they had come without disturbing anything inside. That night they slept peacefully with their bedclothes tucked around their chin. The spirits had left.

A year or so later, after a heavy snowfall in November, the old abandoned house collapsed of its own accord and over time it slowly melted into the tall grass taking its secrets with it.

People still search for the Black Arts Book.

THE DEATH OF WILLIAM HENRY

On the 17th of this month (April)
a man named William Morgan,
with his son, left his home in Lush's Bight.
Two days later he was brought back lifeless,
and his son in a weak condition…

Twillingate Sun, Saturday, June 9, 1888

EASTER Sunday and April Fool's came on the same day in 1888. 'The long hungry month,' as everyone on the coast referred to March, had been a cold one, with three powerful blizzards rocking the Island one after another. March had also brought two full moons, a sure sign to the fishermen of the northeast coast that the stormy unsettled weather would not improve any time soon. Still, there was promise of a new spring as mild southerly winds on this first day of April drove wet snowflakes onto the thin windowpanes of William Henry's modest dwelling.

Winters on the coast were never pleasant but this one seemed the roughest in many years. There had been no let up since the last trader had visited the small community in late October of last year and June would come before the supply schooner, the Plover, returned to outfit fishermen for the summer season. William Henry and his young son, James, had traded their summer's catch, poor as it was, for flour, sugar, tea, lard, and a few other staples. These, along with their harvest from the vegetable gardens and their store of shore fish, would have to see them through the winter.

By the second week of April the mound of potatoes gathered in the fall had dwindled to a single layer on the wooden floor of the root cellar. In the adjoining bin a few yellowed cabbages and some shrivelled turnips were all that remained for the coming months. When the food was gone they would have to seek some help from neighbours but there were only five families in the Bight, all with many children, all struggling to keep life and limb together.

William Henry was now 48 years old and like all hard working family men of the time was somewhat bent by the toil. He had aged beyond his years as he struggled to raise a family of nine children. His wife, Elizabeth, worried endlessly about her husband's health. He seemed to have slowed down these past few years and she encouraged her oldest boy, James, now sixteen, to take on the burden of cutting and hauling the firewood and preparing the gardens for planting.

She worried too that the younger ones weren't getting enough to eat. Heavy snow in the woods this year made it impossible to snare a rabbit for soup. The endless expanse of ice covering the bay meant there was no sea bird to grace the dinner table. Salted Herring had replaced fresh meat.

Around the 15th of April good news came from Ward's Harbour at the eastern end of the Island that some men had been finding seal carcasses on the ice near the Gull Rock. It was rumoured that in late March, the SS Nimrod, a sealing steamer, had run into trouble in the heavy ice off Cape John and her men had to abandon their panned seals. These same floes with their bounty of meat had now drifted towards land on the northeast wind and since the meat and pelts weren't flagged they were any man's property.

With the low temperatures in late March, the heavy Arctic ice that blockaded Notre Dame Bay from Twillingate Long Point to Tilt Cove, had now frozen together into a massive sheet, making it possible for hunters to travel several miles from land in search of the young harps. Such a journey was hazardous at the best of times as the ice heaved and rolled in the ocean swell. Rip tides could suddenly separate the ice sheets, opening wide leads or swatches that left stranded hunters helpless and drifting out to sea. Freak local storms could churn the ocean, sending the massive ice blocks into a frenzy of grinding chaos. At other times the space between sheets of ice was covered with pebbly slush and a false step could mean disaster. From the time they were small boys, leaping from pan to pan in the coves, the hunters had learned the art of manoeuvring over shifting floes, moving quickly with a light foot, knowing precisely where to make the next step, like dancing a jig in the church hall.

William Henry rose early on Tuesday, the 17th of April. Outside it was mild with a light snow falling and a hint of wind from the sou'west, a good day on the ice. From the houses across the harbour the wood smoke was rising straight into the morning air. James had already awakened and dressed by the time his father came down the hallway to tell him they would go for some seals. Elizabeth, too, was up and about, making tea and fretting over the two men.

"Now William Henry, Don't you take no chances and James, you take care of your father," were her parting words as the two left the house.

Ordinarily, her advice would have focused on her son but today she was uneasy without knowing the cause.

Anticipating a long day's walking in mild weather, the two men had decided to dress lightly, wearing woollen overcoats, swanskin pants and sealskin boots. James carried a small lunch bag with hard biscuits and jam. His father carried the old three quarter sealing gun cradled under one arm. Over the eastern hills the sun was trying to break through the snow flurries as they set off across the harbour ice.

They turned north towards the Cape Shore as they rounded Salmon Point. There was a layer of packed snow on the smooth bay ice that had formed in the winter. Walking was easy. But within the hour the snow flurries grew heavier making it difficult to see land no more than a few hundred yards away on the right. They recognized the outline of Kelly's Cove and skirted close to shore around Red Point avoiding the rifted ice over the treacherous shoal just off shore.

The heavy snow had not lifted when they reached the lower Flint Island. James was for turning back to wait for another day. His father's inclination was to wait on the small island for an hour or so until the snow cleared. If there was no change in the weather they would head into Ward's harbour, a half mile away, and stay the night at John Thomas Paddock's place. After resting for a while they could both feel a chill creeping in. Both beat their arms across their chest to warm up. There was no chance of building a fire with the wet driftwood on the small beach so they sat close together sheltered under a rocky outcrop.

By mid-morning the snow had cleared, the cloud cover had lifted, and the sun was breaking through the grey sky. When the two decided to continue, the outline of the Gull Rock was clearly visible 5 miles to the northeast. Further off to the north the Cape Shore was breaking through the morning haze. For a mile out from shore the going was smooth beneath their feet and they made good time but then they met the long barrier where rafted slabs of the heavy arctic floes had come up against the bay ice. They picked their way around and through the obstacle but it was rough going from then on.

The morning quiet was broken only by William Henry's heavy breathing and the occasional call of a crow somewhere on the ice pack. James was now walking in the lead keeping an eye on the spectacle in the eastern sky. A rosy halo had formed around the late morning sun and on either side of the great circle, brilliant orange sun hounds sent sharp pinnacles down to the sea.

"There's weather coming before night." William called after his son, "We'd best be off the ice before dark."

The rough ice had slowed them down considerably. By the time they reached Gull Rock in the early afternoon both wanted a rest and were desperately hungry. The hard biscuit and jam momentarily filled the stomach but their growing thirst was harder to satisfy. Despite the meagre lunch, James felt renewed strength. He climbed to the peak of the small island searching for any sign of seals in the distance. A mile or so to the east he saw several crows hovering and several more appeared to be feeding on the remains of an animal.

Beyond, there was a more startling sight. At the mouth of the bay Cape John Gull Island appeared to be floating on the horizon. Suddenly its appearance changed to that of an anvil almost pinched off in the middle. An upside down steamer, spewing smoke underneath, took shape further out. He thought it must have something to do with the weather but when he described the sight to his father the older man looked worried.

Father and son now decided to strike east towards the

squawking crows. After nearly an hour they found only the wind bleached bones of a seabird. It was then that James' sharp eye noticed a large dark coloured area of sea ice further in the bay towards Little Bay Islands. They both knew it was their last chance for the day. After another hour of trudging through the waning afternoon it was obvious that they had found a treasure trove of meat. There were dozens of seal carcasses strewn over the floe along with several piles of skins, and other animals left untouched. After a long hard day there was success at last and they quickly tied a rope into three seals each and headed back towards Gull Rock.

William Henry had noticed for some time that a sea was making. He grew increasingly uneasy as a barely noticeable swell under the ice sheet earlier in the day had now grown more pronounced as evening neared. The ice pack was starting to break up. A biting northeast wind had also sprung up sending a chill deep into his bones. He summoned all his will power to control the shivering that was taking control of his body. James had noticed the stumble in his father's steps as they neared Gull Rock. He had seen the trembling hand holding the gun and the fleeting look of panic that appeared on the weather beaten face.

"We're just about to the island, father. We'll drop our tow of seals there and head for the Stag Island. There's a warm cabin there and we'll stay the night."

His shaking voice betrayed his panic. They now had no more than half an hour of daylight.

Shelter at the Stag Island was two miles away, a good hour's walk under ideal conditions. But conditions were not ideal and James knew that the distance could double if shifting ice forced them off course. Opposite the Middle Islands the wind seemed to pick up, bringing with it a steady driving snow which bit into their faces. Swatches of dark water opened up with the ocean swell. They detoured around some and twice had to use their gaffs to manoeuvre across the leads on moving ice pans.

William Henry had stopped shivering but complained of being cold and weak. His feet felt heavy.

"Where are we, son, and where's our seals?"

James could barely make out the slurred words. He tried to get his father to eat a biscuit.

"We dropped the seals off on the Gull Rock, father. We'll be at the cabin in half an hour and we'll get a fire going."

James' reassuring words did not seem to register. He noticed that his father no longer carried the sealing gun.

Fifteen yards from Stag Island Point a greater danger confronted the two men. The swell, the wind and the undertow had joined forces to create a treacherous whirlpool of ice and foam. They moved cautiously down-wind from the mist shrouded lead, hoping to find a safer approach to land.

It happened in a flash and yet as James was to describe later it seemed all in slow motion; the ice giving way under his father's feet; the sudden moan; the older man reaching out with his gaff; the gaff missing its mark and sticking into his upper leg. James reached out in time to hook his father by the collar before the whirling mass took him under. With great effort James pulled him back on a solid pan and got him standing. This time he grabbed his father's arm but had no sooner done so when the ice gave way again. The shock of the cold ocean water had now sapped William Henry's strength. He could no longer stand but summoning some inner strength he crawled to the icy rocks on the shoreline.

James knew that another obstacle course awaited

them on shore, a jumble of slick batty-catters. This icy barrier of shore fast ice was formed above the low water mark by the ebb and flow of the tides. During the winter months pans of broken sea ice would wash up, become grounded and freeze into the previous layer. Over time a jumbled mass of jagged chunks and deep fissures formed. Only a sure footed man would attempt to walk through and over the hummocks. Unable to get a good footing, James pulled his father over a small ridge but he lost his grip and William Henry rolled back down into the icy water between the batty-catters. Again he was able to pull him back up with his gaff. His father had now become delirious and James could only understand the sound of his own name and the words, "We shall all sleep together."

James, himself, was now exhausted by the effort and felt the effects of the cold seeping through his own damp clothing. He tried to ward off his growing panic by recalling what the old ones had said about these situations. He cradled his father to a sitting position and tried holding him close to his own body to provide some warmth but William Henry's icy clothing was a barrier to the body heat. He thought of removing his father's stiff overcoat but then he would be totally exposed to the driving snow and wind. He tried moving his father's arms in a beating motion to generate heat but the arms were stiff and there was little response.

With a supreme effort he managed to drag the near lifeless body to a more sheltered spot behind a rafted ice sheet. They were out of the wind but the two men were again on glassy ice with a noticeable slope down to the land-wash. This time James stretched his father out and lay close beside him hoping that by some miracle his own determination to survive would seep into the limp body he embraced. Perhaps, if he prayed...but the words would not come.

After lying beside his father for what seemed like endless hours, painful cramps began to develop in his shoulders and legs. He moved slightly to change his position. The small movement caused the unconscious man to roll back into a deep water filled crevasse on the shoreline. James screamed and hauled on the rope he had tied around his father's shoulders but this time he could not summon the strength. William Henry sighed softly, breathed his last, and slid back into the icy blackness. James wedged his gaff upright in a narrow crevice and fastened his father's body as best he could.

He stayed for a long time contemplating the scene, overcome with grief and fear by the tragedy that had unfolded. Finally his reason returned and he realized that the hunters' cabins must be about a quarter mile to the south in Stag Island Harbour. He would have to get there or suffer the same fate as his father.

James now embarked on a superhuman effort to find the shelter he knew was on the island. He crawled slowly up the slick barrier to a stand of low trees which offered a buffer to the northeast wind and blowing snow. It was as much as his weakened body could manage. He burrowed down, stretched out and fell asleep. Sometime during the night he recalled awakening, eating a little clammy snow, and lapsing back into a deep slumber.

It was the feel of the snow on his face that awakened him early on Wednesday morning. He thought at first he must somehow be at home and it was all a nightmare. A glance down to the shoreline confirmed his predicament. The cold and dampness had numbed his legs all the way to his toes but the intense burning pain in his feet indicated they were not yet frozen. He tried standing but soon realized that he would have to crawl to the cabins.

It was a slow painful journey over the sparsely wooded

hills but within two hours James could make out the north beach. Just over the rise on the south side there was shelter. In another hour he had found a cabin and then a crushing disappointment; there was no food or bedclothes of any kind. There was no way of making a fire. He collapsed on the floor and drifted in and out of a dream state.

When he regained his senses he prayed for deliverance. Surprised at the strength of his own voice, and, convinced of a miracle, he discovered he could stand up. He spotted the second cabin barely twenty yards away and stumbled through the snow towards the door. Inside there was deliverance in the form of heavy blankets on the bunks and food on the shelf. He found matches but these were too damp to ignite. He ate, took off his wet clothing, crawled underneath the heavy bedding and slept.

James awoke late into Thursday morning to the sound of men's voices outside the cabin. The door opened and John Thomas Paddock walked in.

"How did you get here, my boy?"

The soft tone of his voice brought a rush of tears and a torrent of emotion as James described what had transpired over the past two days. The men lit a roaring fire to warm the cabin and then prepared hot food and tea. As James dressed he noticed for the first time his lacerated and bleeding knees. His swanskin trousers and underpants were worn through and tattered all the way to his ankles.

John Thomas sent his eight companions to retrieve the body of the man that was William Henry.

STILL WATERS

The floating cities came and took the fish.
The landlocked cities took the children.
And like the Beothuk we too will disappear from the island.

FRANKIE thought that even his grandfather's old horse, Bob, knew that he was leaving. It had broken off from the herd roaming the meadows late in the evening and wandered back begging for some molasses bread at the kitchen window. The ancient animal had stayed around looking forlorn. Finally Frankie had shown it to the barn stall for the night.

He was leaving the island. Of that, there was no doubt. His mother had long since decided that not one child would stay.

"You're nothing without an education," she would say, "because there's no future in the fishery," and then a deep sigh as she looked around to make sure all the children were listening.

His father made it equally plain that there was always a place for one more in the boat.

"That's one more for the fishing grounds," he would announce each time the mid-wife emerged from the bedroom to announce that another healthy child was born.

His mother and father were like that, he thought, opposites of each other. She, forever impatient at having to make do with nothing but a thirty dollar family allowance and not a sup of orange juice in the house, always on the thin edge of poverty, making bread four times a week to fill all the empty stomachs; His father, at peace with the world, always with the belief that things would get better, the fish would strike in next week, there'd be a better price for turbot by and by..."if the Russians don't blow us all to hell before then".

Things had gone downhill even further this year. There was plenty of salmon but no market, plenty of lobster at a lousy price. There was, however, a good demand for pickled turbot. His father had packed nearly fifty barrels for market being careful to use the recommended amount of brine. He then stored the barrels carefully in the ballast bed underneath the wharf where it was cool. The inspector had come in early August to check the shipment. As he carefully popped the top of each barrel there was a low hiss of escaping gas and a rotten fish smell. The whole lot had spoiled and a summer's work was dumped over the wharf. The blow had shrunk his father and he aged ten years in a month.

"We've got a dead man's share from this summer's voyage," commented his mother bitterly.

"You're born, you suffer, you die, fortunately, there's a loophole, that's what Billy said," observed his father, quoting Billy Graham.

For weeks his father retreated into his own secluded world trying to come to terms with the ultimate shame of having to go on board the government boat the next time the welfare officer visited. The boat landed at the merchant's wharf across the harbour a week later, and one by one, men from around the Island slowly made their way towards it. They took casual detours along the main road to hide their true intentions, admiring Bessie's cabbage patch, talking about the weather, trying to be invisible.

Frankie's mother had pressed on, not caring anymore where the food money came from. The sad little Jewish pedlar, smelling of camphor in his shabby suit, had shown up again with his heavy suitcases asking whether he could set up in the parlour for the day. He unpacked his merchandise and laid it out around the room: cheap costume jewellery, calico blouses, white handkerchiefs, bright bandannas and rainbow-coloured little girl's dresses; tea aprons, nylons, daintily embroidered muslin and hats for the church ladies. His mother sat proudly in her rocking chair with a carefree smile, basking in the glow of the pedlar's wares. Mothers from around the harbour came to look, to haggle, and sometimes to grudgingly buy an item that caught the eye. She gave the pedlar some fried fish for lunch and as he was leaving in mid-afternoon he handed over a bolt of cheap flannelette for her troubles.

Much too soon, Frankie was finished with school on the Island and was the next in the family line to leave, having just been accepted for a program at the university in far off St. John's. The letter had come just a week ago. At that late date it would take a miracle to find enough money to get to the city and pay the registration fees as well as the first month's board.

But a miracle had happened and he now sat in the tiny kitchen in the early morning with his small suitcase at his feet. He waited for the arrival of the coastal ferry, Northern Ranger, to take him to Lewisporte where he would catch the train to the city. The slight bulge of the precious envelope in his inside coat pocket took the edge off the creeping loneliness and the rising panic at having to leave home.

His mother, her knitting needles stabbing intensely into the unfinished toe of a wool sock, sat at the big table in the kitchen with a satisfied look on her face, mouthing words without sound. She did that, when she was content, keeping her hands busy, rummaging through her mother thoughts, and carrying on some secret inner conversation.

His father, with his sea worn face and salty, ocean smell, sat impassively slurping his hot tea, pouring it methodically from his cup into the saucer, shrugging every now and then as if shaking seaweed from his shoulders, keeping his thoughts to himself. No words were spoken.

Uncle Sim came by spreading the latest news into the early morning, knocking mud from the end of his peg leg as he came in the door, chewing on a wad of tobacco. He sat by the woodstove lifting the cover every few minutes to release a mouthful of black juice into the flames.

"Chiang Kai-shek was up to his old tricks again in Formosa…He'll go back and take China from the Communists one of these days…The Russians shot down that American spy plane…That old Diefenbaker is nothing but a strife breeder… We need Winston Churchill back."

"Watch out in St. John's, my son. They're a hard crowd in there, a lot of Catholics!"

The deep mournful sound of the ship's whistle interrupted the conversation.

"I'll take you over to the government wharf in the boat," said his father as they stood to go.

"Be careful", were the parting words from his mother.

The old Northern Ranger, a relic of the 1930's, had seen better times. Rust, thinly disguised with a coat of paint, was eating its way through much of the deck machinery and a large brown stain ran down from the anchor ports on the ship's bow. Clouds of black diesel belched from the smoke stack leaning from the upper deck. On the inside the ship still retained some splendour from its glory days

with a well-appointed dining salon and comfortable passenger cabins. Frankie went to the ship's office to pay his
fare.

"Six dollars to Lewisporte," shouted the purser above
the deck noise, "for another dollar you can have a bunk
and two meals. We don't get in until noon tomorrow."

The overpowering smell of bilge water from below and
stale kitchen grease from the open galley door made him
queasy. He handed over a ten dollar bill, a good chunk of
what he had managed to save from selling lobster at the
end of the season. He pocketed the change and went back
outside.

On deck Frankie moved away from the knot of passengers still buying tickets and carefully checked the inside pocket of his jacket to make sure the envelope full
of money was still there. He rubbed each crisp ten and
twenty dollar bill between his fingers, looking at each one
in turn, counting up the total and pressing the pocket
closed again. He looked around to make sure no one was
watching.

The old ship sounded a short grunt on its whistle and
backed away from the wharf. Frankie noticed the old
church sitting proudly on the Meetinghouse Point, keeping watch over its flock, guarding their secrets behind its
stained glass windows.

Frankie thought of his fright years ago, when his father sent him to light the wood stoves on a frigid Sunday
morning in January. While he was waiting for the place
to warm up he'd decided to dig some pennies out of the
cracks in the window sill with his new Roy Rogers pocket knife. He had no sooner stuck the blade into the soft
wood when a loud crash sounded behind the pulpit, the
front door flew open, a cold wind filled the pews. He had
run from the place in terror. He'd always had the strange

feeling that the building was alive somehow, that it had emotions like him and it only felt happy when it was full of people.

On the starboard side Gid, the movie man, was steaming into the harbour with his juke box rigged to a dry cell battery and a loud speaker blaring 'Deep in the Heart of Texas.' Gid waved goodbye when he spotted Frankie on deck, shouting something that was lost in the wind. It carried Frankie back a dozen years to a simpler time when he did not have to make decisions or worry about what lay in store down the road.

HE remembered when the Lone Ranger came to the Island with Tonto, his noble partner in the never ending fight against the outlaws of the Wild West. No longer would Frankie have to listen to the exploits of that masked man on the radio, missing key parts of the story as the radio signal gurgled in and out from the New York station. No longer would he have to read comic books to relive his hero's exploits. Not only was the Lone Ranger coming but he was coming twice, a rare double feature in living Technicolor. Admission was only twenty-five cents, two for the price of one. Even the teacher seemed excited and for the first time announced there would be a movie on Friday night but he refused to be drawn into a discussion about who the masked man was despite the urgent questions from the boys and girls. The class went back to the dreary task of long division.

On Wednesday, Gid, the movie man, landed from across the bay and put up the movie poster in the tiny lobby of the post office. The picture itself caused a mob scene as everyone crowded in to see the legendary masked man in the saddle, his pearl handled six shooters and studded gun belt filled with silver bullets, his great white stallion, Silver, rearing on its two hind legs. And there beside him

looking on adoringly was Tonto, his faithful Indian companion, with his hair braided in two long braids.

There was much pushing, shoving and shouting as
Frankie and his friends crowded in to see the poster of
their hero until finally, the post mistress, in a fit of temper, shushed everybody out of the lobby suggesting they
should all go home so their mothers could teach them better sense. She took the poster down and nailed it to the
outside door with her stamper. The rain on Thursday
leached away the colour till there was nothing left but
the Lone Ranger's mask and for a long twenty four hours
there was no release for the children's pent up tension
and excitement.

Frankie spent Friday after school hauling water from
the well for his grandmother who always rewarded him
with the quarter he would need for admission to the mov-
ies. By seven thirty every seat was taken and late comers
were standing in the back. Frankie went directly to the
front and squeezed in beside Rosie and her three boys.

The shades were drawn and the room went quiet as the
projector whirred into motion and the speakers crackled
with static. The stirring music of the William Tell Over-
ture brought the Lone Ranger and Tonto galloping at full
speed towards the audience, their horses reared and the
masked one let out a "Hi Yo, Silver, Away", and the fiery
horse with the speed of light and a cloud of dust sped
towards town. Some outlaws who had captured a pretty
woman got the drop on Tonto and threatened to plug him
with lead but the next instant 'Kemo Sabe' sprang from
cover with six guns blazing and rescued his faithful partner. The outlaws ran away.

Gid threaded 'The Lone Ranger Rides Again' on the
projector but it started badly with many breaks. Finally
he abandoned the effort and explained to the audience

that he would have to show another feature.

"The Wild Women of Wongo", "a popular film in Canada", he said.. "…on a faraway tropical island," Gid read from the poster, "lived a tribe of beautiful women, on the other side an evil ape clan looking for mates…"

Some angry mothers suspected the film was not fit for Christian eyes and demanded their money back before leaving with their children in tow.

THE Northern Ranger was well into the run when Frankie broke from his daydream and allowed the loneliness to seep back in. White water splashed along the sides of the ship and a brisk westerly wind finally ushered him off the deck. He held his jacket tightly to his chest. It was getting close to dinner and he would have to find a seat at a table. He touched his jacket pocket again and moved with a shy, hesitant step towards the galley.

He stopped in the dining room doorway staring nervously at the clean white linens on tables set with gleaming silverware. As he turned away from the intimidating sight, a steward motioned him forward to sit at a table with two older men who introduced themselves as merchants from across the bay. The steward told him what was being served but Frankie remembered nothing in his flustered state and simply nodded a yes, hoping that it was the correct answer. Momentarily, the young man reappeared with a tray of steaming bowls.

"We've got some nice ox-tail soup for you this evening," he commented as he set a bowl beside each person.

Frankie had never heard of such a thing and nervously poked at the bony meat sections with his spoon, a vision of a cow's tail in his head. Hunger soon overcame his hesitation and he dove into the tasty soup.

After dinner, Frankie went back on deck, moving away

from the windward side of the ship. Darkness had fallen
and the blackness of the sea was broken only by the occasional whitecap and by the ship's long wake stringing
out behind. On the port side the silent outline of the Island was fading into the night. He recognized some of the
fishing grounds and imagined his father's boat with the
burden of the deep water trawl weighing down its bow
and the unending string of cod emerging from the depths.

"The only time father was happy, was when he was on
the water," thought Frankie.

The man turned into a different person on the sea. Out
here on the ocean he brimmed with confidence. He was
ten feet tall. He seemed to grow when he stepped in the
boat. It was almost as if he was a sea creature himself,
knowing where the lobsters hid and the large cod swam,
and when the fat Atlantic Salmon ran headlong for the
rivers. Every morning his father opened the front door of
his home, looked into the sky, spat into the approaching
dawn, and announced what the weather would be on the
ocean that day.

On land he was someone else. He raged against the
politicians on the radio who told fishermen to burn their
boats.

"Two jobs for every man..." the premier shouted over
the airwaves.

"Should be shot," responded his father, nodding at the
framed picture of the famous man his wife had hung on
the kitchen wall.

In the end he seemed to give up on the news altogether
unless it was something about fish. On Sundays he listened to the silver tongued evangelist, Billy Graham, on
the radio, quoting him for the rest of the week in the fishing boat and sometimes retelling Billy's stories.

"Do you know what Sir Walter Raleigh said when they

were chopping his head off?" asked his father as they pulled the nets aboard. It was a roundabout way of telling his favourite Billy story.

"The officer asked him if his head lay right. And Sir Walter said 'It matters not how the head lies as long as the heart is right.' Billy told that story," explained his father proudly.

After the rousing sermon and the choir led by George Beverly Shea began the hymns, his father always napped on the daybed in the parlour.

During those times the old hag came to visit him as he dozed peacefully on the quiet Sunday afternoons. He could see the dark form enter the parlour and move ominously towards him on the bed, climbing onto his chest. It perched there, black and faceless, like a giant vulture with its wings hanging loosely by its sides. He heard the children in the next room and tried to call out to his wife close by, but no sound came from his lips. He tried moving his fingers or his toes but the old hag had paralysed him and he realised he was neither awake nor asleep. Anyone close by could see his lips slightly shivering, trying to form words, his eyes darting in terror behind his eyelids. Sometimes he struggled free after a mighty effort of stubborn will and woke up with a scream and a curse. At other times a child touched him lightly on the shoulder and he groaned gratefully for his deliverance from evil. Invariably, he fell back into deep slumber and the unequal battle resumed.

He only went to one movie in his whole life, recalled Frankie, and that was when he had convinced his father that Gid was showing a Second World War film he shouldn't miss. They sat together in the middle row with Frankie continually glancing at his father's face. 'War of the Worlds' turned out to be a disaster with weird Martians crawling all over a devastated earth. His father walked out in disgust after the first reel.

By midnight the open sea had spread its chill along the deck of the coastal boat and Frankie went inside to find his bunk. He again checked his inside pocket and carefully folded his jacket before placing it under the pillow. During the night the heavy throbbing of the ships motors kept him in a restless sleep. In his dreams he was back in his own bedroom with its sad window facing the wooded hills instead of the sea, and the timid south wind moaning around the sash.

It was the same every morning during the fishing season. When his father came to wake him he could hear the heavy measured footsteps coming down the hallway and the sound always made him think that the man carried all his weight in his feet.

Afterwards, he could hear his father down below in the kitchen turning the radio dial in the darkness of early morning searching for WWVA, Wheeling, West Virginia with its 50,000 watt transmitter booming its message all the way to the Island. The signal faded in and out until the silky southern voice of Lee Moore, the coffee-drinking night hawk, grew louder, finishing the last verse of 'The Cat Came Back,' his father's favourite song. Lee launched into an ad for a tablecloth showing the Last Supper.

"A beautiful embroidered picture of Jesus and the twelve disciples...a free set of table napkins each with a disciple's face... just send ten dollars to me, Lee Moore, doublya, doublya, Vee Ay..." as he strummed his guitar and talked to Jaunita, his gal from the Blue Ridge Mountains, sitting beside him in the studio.

In his dream Frankie was sitting at the breakfast table drinking black tea as Lee Moore and Jaunita sang

'Keep on the Sunny Side.'

Frankie awakened with a start and adjusted to his surroundings as the ship's motors kicked into reverse and the purser knocked on the door to announce the arrival in Leading Tickles. It was five in the morning, another three hours before breakfast. They would be in Lewisporte by early afternoon.

In his new dream Frankie was looking overboard into the clear still water of the harbour as he and his father steamed out to the nets in the early morning. A dead dog, its hind leg attached to a cement block on the harbour bottom, appeared to be running diagonally towards the boat, its snout pointed forward as if it were racing to the surface. His father had noticed it too and swung the boat around to take another look.

"It doesn't belong there, a blasphemy," he was shouting above the noise of the motor, "we'll have to take it ashore and bury it."

The dream made no sense after that but Frankie was finished with sleep for the morning.

He sat for breakfast, uneasily contemplating the silverware and the place setting, two forks, two spoons, a gleaming knife, and a carefully folded linen serviette. Only one of the merchants from the night before was sitting at the breakfast table and he inquired about Frankie's destination. Frankie mumbled something about university but didn't have the words for long conversation.

"That's the best thing for young people," offered his companion, "You can have any job you want then."

"I wanted to join the army," responded Frankie, hoping to impress the man, "But my mother didn't want me to go up to Canada."

"Have you been away from home before?" asked the man.

"Only to Springdale a few times to the hospital," replied Frankie in a low voice.

"I'll help you get on the train," offered his companion,
"Because it's a little complicated, you have to take one
train up to the junction and then get on the Express to
St. John's."

The man's offer relieved Frankie's increasing uneasi-
ness. The steward came with small glasses of orange juice
and inquired how they liked their eggs.

"Easy over," responded the merchant.

"I'll have the same," Frankie said, not knowing what
'easy over' meant in relation to eggs.

"I'm just going to Lewisporte to meet the wholesalers,"
said the merchant, turning his attention back to Frankie.
"I hope I can catch the Ranger back tomorrow morning."

The plates came, neatly arranged with long slices of
crisp bacon, soft fried eggs and hot buttered toast. He
watched to see which fork his companion would pick up.

"You'll have a few hours to wander around Lewisporte," suggested the merchant. The train doesn't go up
to the junction until four. Pick up something to read. It'll
be twelve hours or more to St. John's."

The Northern Ranger pulled into the CN dock shortly
after noon. Ahead, Frankie saw the big orange and green
engine with its two passenger coaches strung on behind
waiting at the station. The merchant took him across
the busy dock to the ticket office, explaining to the agent
where Frankie was going.

"Departure for the Junction at 5 PM," said the agent
as Frankie passed him the twenty–two dollar fare. "The
express leaves at 6:30."He still had eleven dollars in his
pocket, he thought, without having to touch the bills in
the envelope.

He wandered around the busy town for several hours,

walking on pavement for the first time, marvelling at a movie poster for 'The Guns of Navarone', buying the Star Weekly and a ham sandwich at Manuel's Hotel. Strangers brushed by without acknowledging his presence, looking past him at some unseen destination even when he said hello.

By the time he boarded the train, the little station was crowded with people. Parents waved goodbye to their sons and daughters who were leaving, like him, for the big city.

Small groups of youngsters, some holding fishing rods, stood staring at the slowly moving train. A gaggle of young people his own age noisily changed seats around him, girls trying to sit by each other or besides fawning boyfriends. They chattered in shrill excitement about Elvis while Frankie self-consciously kept his eyes on the trees rushing by as the train picked up speed.

The express had already run an hour late by the time the whistle sounded its arrival at the junction and darkness had fallen by the time the new passengers from Lewisporte boarded. The train staggered forward and then backward with a loud clang as a new coach was added somewhere in the rear. Then with a long mournful blast it lurched forward again and slowly moved from the station. A conductor came through chatting easily with passengers and punching holes in their tickets.

"Dining car is four coaches down, open until ten. Enjoy your trip."

A steward came through selling pop, chocolate bars and chips. Frankie bought a bottle of orange crush to wash down his ham sandwich.

"Glenwood," called the conductor as he walked through the car an hour later, "Gander, next."

A girl with a small suitcase took the seat next to him

in Glenwood. They shyly exchanged names and talked about where they were going but the conversation died out quickly. He hoped he would have the courage to ask for her address before they got to the city.

The coach was just about full after leaving Gander where a merry group of returning students spilled in and occupied the seats across the aisle from Frankie. They brought out a guitar and passed a bottle of lemon gin back and forth keeping an eye out for the conductor who returned after the train pulled away to check their tickets.

"Enjoy yourselves," he said. "But you'll have to keep it down after twelve."

"Hit the road Jack," they sang in a semblance of loud harmony, "and don't you come back, no more, no more, no more, no more."

It was like listening to the top 40, thought Frankie as they launched into "Momma said there'd be days like this, days like this, momma said..." He realized the entertainment was taking the edge off his homesickness and the rhythm of the train made him sleepy.

ARNIE Ginsberg was coming in loud and clear from WMEX in Boston. He'd turned the volume as low as possible so his father wouldn't wake up.

"Arnie Woo Woo Ginsberg," the DJ announced, pulling on a train whistle, "Old aching adenoids, himself, playing all the hit records especially for you. Hey kids, if you're ever craving a burger, head on out to the Adventure Car Hop, Route one, in Saugus. Ask for a Ginsburger, tell them Arnie sent you and get another one free."

"Goobies, next stop," shouted the conductor trying to make himself heard above the noise.

Frankie woke with a start. Everyone was singing

'Does Your Chewing Gum Lose its Flavour on the Bedpost Overnight...'After Goobies the coach went quiet for the rest of the long night. Frankie was barely conscious of other stops along the way and only woke with the train moving along an ocean front after stopping in Holyrood.

"Ninety minutes to St. John's," announced the conductor, "Foxtrap, next stop."

He checked his pocket again and thought about his father's surprise. He'd gone to bed three nights ago with a helpless feeling knowing that there was no hope of going away this year. Even the government grant wouldn't be enough. Besides it wouldn't be available until sometime late in October. His father had called him as usual early next morning even though they both knew they wouldn't be fishing that day. WWVA came in loud and clear. Lee Moore and Jaunita were singing 'Wildwood Flower.'

Then his father had handed him the envelope filled with bills.

"It ought to get you through," he said, "I told the welfare officer the co-op shares were in your name just so he wouldn't think I was crooked. I changed them all over last week."

There was silence in the kitchen but he sensed the meaning in his father's gesture.

Frankie's landlady was at the station on Water Street to greet him. She got him into a taxi.

"10 Brazil Square," she said.

Frankie stared out the taxi window as they drove along Water Street. He thought he heard his father's voice.

"Do you know what Billy Graham said?" asked his father. "I've read the last page of my Bible, and everything turns out all right. Billy said that."

LEVI'S WAR

I must tell you about my son, Levi. His name is really and truly Levi Caravan but when a small boy when I married James I had to put him out for peace as James had boys of his own.

from Annie's Letter to Lieut. Col. Rendell,
Royal Newfoundland Regiment July 23, 1918.

LEVI was born to a single mother, Annie Eliza, on a cold winter's day in the final weeks of October, 1890. He was christened Levi Caravan in early December. Normally at this time of year people were looking forward to a Christmas season filled with community celebrations, with dancing and mummering, to a time of joy and rebirth.

This year it was to be a muted celebration of families stalked by the dreaded killer, diphtheria, which had been ravaging villages all along the northeast coast for over five years and was now reaching its peak. During that time more than thirty children had died on the Island. The deadly disease was highly contagious and by order of the Dominion's Health Department stricken families were quarantined while others were strongly advised to avoid gatherings of more than three or four people. Against all odds Levi survived.

Annie was 31 years of age when Levi was born. As soon as the baby arrived she faced considerable challenges as a single parent in a straight laced Methodist community.

The child was born out of wedlock. Mortal sin, it was, and fodder for endless gossip. She would now have to provide for herself and her child in a home where her parents were already overburdened and barely able to provide for themselves. There was no social assistance and no health care aside from folk medicine. There were no job prospects for any young woman much less a single mother.

Despite the conditions, Levi thrived as an infant, and as a male child, he had a privileged position in the household. With uncommon determination Annie struggled to make ends meet. Living with her elderly parents and without a supporting husband the outlook was grim.

In October of 1892 when Levi was 22 months old, Annie and her parents received a visit from James, a widower, who had recently lost his wife to diphtheria. James described his own hardships trying to hold together a family of four active boys while making a living at the same time. Herb was 13 years old and could get by on his own but Titus, Sim, and Wilson were mere boys and needed a mother's care. For the past five months since the death of their mother they had been looked after by another family. This was a temporary arrangement and they would have to return home to Island Cove for the winter.

The marriage proposal was matter of fact, passionless and practical, a favour to Annie. James would marry her but as Annie feared there was a condition. She could not bring Levi into the marriage. He would have to remain with Annie's parents or be adopted out. Annie was to admit later in a statement of supreme irony that her decision to give him out for adoption was "to keep the peace".

Well, Mr. John Normore wanted to adopt him as his own son and to call him by their name. But I was not satisfied for him to have his name any other than Levi Caravan what

he was baptized by Rev. Mr. Russell of Exploits. Neither did
we have any writings of any sort only the word of mouth
that if they treat him fairly I would not trouble them until
he would be 21 years of age and out of his time…
                    From Annie's letter to Lieut. Col. Rendell.

LEVI was to spend his second Christmas in Wellman's
Cove on Sunday Cove Island and only a short distance
from his birthplace. It was a traumatic separation for
the mother and equally traumatic for the child after 22
months of devoted attention. The child's new parents
were John and Dinah Normore. They had chosen him as
their son and as a new brother and companion for their
youngest daughter, Bertha, who was ten year old at the
time. Since their other children, Martha and George were
grown and making homes of their own John and Dinah
also needed the security that a young son could provide
in their old age.

Wellman's Cove was a very different environment from
that of Long Island. Its people worked small farms, raised
cows and sheep and looked more to the land as the source
of their livelihood to supplement their meagre living from
the sea. Well worn trails from Wellmans Cove led to other
small communities on Sunday Cove Island. Growing up
in this pastoral environment Levi walked these trails, at
times glancing at Long Island just a few kilometres to the
east, unaware of his birth connection.

He would have had little time to contemplate his ori-
gins as his new father, John, died around 1895 and, in the
absence of schooling, childhood quickly blended into adult-
hood. Levi was soon expected to shoulder the burden of support for his sister Bertha and his adoptive mother, Dinah.

The 20th Century began much as the last one had
ended. There was optimism at the dawn of a new scien-
tific age but the seeds of conflict were evident with every

scrap of news from the outside world. France, Germany, Russia, Great Britain, and a host of minor powers were vying for lands and influence beyond their borders. The savagery of the Boer War had begun in 1899 and would last for another three years. In a little over a dozen years these great powers would be involved in the bloodiest conflict in recorded history.

The Normore family struggled for another eight years in Wellman's Cove, supported by Levi who had now grown into a wiry young man with energy to burn and adventure in his soul. He was fun loving and out-going, but a young man in search of an identity. By 1908 it was time to move to a larger community with better opportunities.

Bertha left first to marry Andrew Hewlett in Wards Harbour and within several years both Levi and Dinah had joined Bertha in her new home. With closer access to good fishing grounds Andrew and Levi made enough to survive but their account was forever in the red with Strong & Murcell, the merchants at Little Bay Islands.

In a break from long established tradition, Levi carried with him a desire to explore the unknown, to try something other than the fishery. He wanted ready cash in his pocket, something he would never have with a merchant account.

The local Notre Dame Bay newspaper, The Twillingate Sun, often carried stories about Newfoundlanders finding work in the coal mines of Cape Breton. At a time when prospects were not bright in the fishery Levi had contacted the coal company in early January to enquire about work. They had responded with an offer of a job in Glace Bay.

In 1911 the Dominion Coal Company in Glace Bay was actively seeking workers to replace those that had begun a bitter strike against the company twenty-two months

previously. The armed militia had been called in to pro-
tect company property, machine gun nests were set up,
striking workers and their families were evicted from
company housing and denied food from company stores.
The mine sites were seething cauldrons of resentment,
anger, and starving families. Workers from Newfoundland were engaged to replace those blacklisted by the
company.

> *...well, after he was 21 years old he left the Normores and
> went to Cape Britten(sic) and spent a year or two there and
> then he came back and settled down on this island...*
>
> from Annie's letter to Lieut. Col. Rendell.

IN late April of that year Levi engaged Andrew to take
him by dog team over the shifting sea ice from Long Island, a treacherous journey made even more so by an early spring thaw. They picked their way over the frozen run
through Sunday Cove Tickle, to South Brook and along
the Halls Bay line to Badger. He then caught the Reid
Newfoundland train to Port Aux Basques.

It was normally a lonely journey across a forested wil-
derness along the Exploits and over the Gaff Topsails.
Many other young men were making the same journey,
Andrew Cuff from Wesleyville, William Morgan from Bay
Roberts, Andrew Tilley from St. John's and several others
from the south coast. Altogether eight young men were
seeking a more secure livelihood beyond the depressed
outports of the island. Through the night they sang the
old songs and exchanged stories, awakening next morning adjacent to the dock in Port Aux Basques.

The last leg of the journey was to be on the steam ferry, Invermore, recently assigned to the Gulf run after the
sinking of the Bruce only a month earlier. They boarded
the ship with their second class tickets along with a hun-

dred others on their way to Canada and the United States in search of a brighter future. Compared to the fishing schooners they had been used to, this was a massive and luxurious vessel.

After a smooth run across the Gulf, Levi and his fellow travellers passed through Canada Immigration and were met by a dour, tough looking company official. He informed them he was to take them to the Glace Bay Mine, sign them on, and show them the ropes. The company train wound its way through a blackened countryside the twelve miles to the mine site. As they wound their way through the workers' village they saw the hostile stares of ragged men, and the vacant eyes of their women and children standing outside shacks along the rail line. The boisterous optimism of the last two days was now replaced with a growing unease.

Inside the main gate of Dominion Colliery Number Three the men were taken into a one room coal shack where the conditions and rules of work were laid out by the foreman: They must never associate with a member of the United Mine Workers of America; They must not support any action against The Dominion Coal Company. They would be required to work in teams with a mini-mum production quota of six tons per day and anything less would be deducted from the $2.60 daily wage. Bunk-house and meal costs were to be deducted from pay every two weeks. All personal items and extra food must be purchased at the company store on site. This too would be deducted from pay as would medical expenses and dona-tions to the church whether they attended or not.

The men were issued their rudimentary mining tools, a pick, a hammer and wedge, a drill and a bucket filled with blasting powder. After several hours of instruction they were ready for the deeps. Nothing could have pre-pared the young men for the crushing reality of working in the damp blackness of the mine where the sharp oily scent of the underground tunnels mixed with the smell of manure and sweating horses. In the dim light of their carbide lamps they picked at the coal seam with steel bars. Massive chunks of coal were loosened and loaded by hand on carts which were pulled by pit ponies to the main trolley line.

With every breath they sucked the dust laden air of the coal mine into their lungs. It clogged the nose and clung to the mouth and throat. After a few hours their faces were blackened in the thin air of the drift. The long days were filled with the endless drudgery of the mine and the back breaking work of loading cars. The routine varied little from week to week and month to month.

Levi watched as fellow miners were crippled or killed by collapsing shafts and miscalculated blasts. In one such incident Levi and his partner had drilled into a half completed bore hole that had been partially charged. While the resulting explosion was small it left both men with face wounds that needed medical attention.

Several youngsters, no more than fourteen, had been torn to pieces when they fell underneath coal cars. Older miners merely postponed a slow, painful, and inevitable death. They coughed endlessly, releasing a black spit tinged with blood as their lungs struggled to loosen the growing film of coal dust. Their lives dimmed with each descent into the mine.

In late spring of 1913 Dominion Coal announced new wage cuts and the Provincial Workman's Association, representing the workers, caved to company demands. A disillusioned Levi collected his paltry earnings from the pay office and walked the 12 miles to North Sydney to arrange passage back to Newfoundland.

It had been two years of near enslavement where or-

dinary workers were treated little better than the pit ponies that worked beside them. With each payday Levi's
pay statement showed an exact match between his wages
and his deductions for board, lodging, and general items.

The streets of North Sydney were another world. People talked about the loss by The Sydney Millionaires to
the Quebec Bulldogs in the Stanley Cup final. The Cape
Breton Post carried front page headlines on the Balkan
War and its implication for peace in Europe. Greek, Ser-
bian, and Romanian troops were massing for an assault
on Bulgaria. Britain, Germany, Russia, and France were
taking sides. Woodrow Wilson was inaugurated as the
28th President of the United States. Sydney stores carried tobacco and other items at half the cost in the company store in Glace Bay.

Levi caught the SS Kyle to Port Aux Basques and
made the return trip across the island by train to Lewisporte where he was able to book passage on the SS Clyde.
It was the first trip of the season for the coastal boat after
a long delay caused by ice floes blocking the coast all the
way from Labrador to St. John's. The journey along the
coast was an opportunity to breathe the fresh salt air of
the ocean as they visited the sheltered communities of
Twillingate, Leading Tickles, Triton Harbour and Pilley's
Island. The old steamer left cargoes of precious food supplies at each stop along the way.

At this time of year all the harbours were hives of
activity as fishermen readied their gear for the frenzied
months of activity ahead. They rounded Southern Head,
at the east end of Long Island on a mild June morning
with a light wind hinting at rain. Several massive ice
bergs were suspended in low fog banks near the steep
cliffs of Croucher's Bight. Just ahead was Cutwell Harbour where Levi was met by Bertha, Andrew and a host

of other friendly faces crowding the wharf as the steamer docked.

Andrew and Bertha's small home was now getting crowded with the addition of three children in the past three years and another on the way. But Bertha, ever the attentive sister, had arranged a comfortable boarding house with the merchant Ken Short and his wife, Mary.

In return for meals and lodging Levi provided much of the manual labour for the business and the family. Vegetable gardens were set and caplin hauled and spread for fertilizer. Freight was moved from wharf to store every time the Clyde arrived. Supplies were delivered to families along the waterfront.

Despite these demands he was able to become a shareman on a trap skiff owned by Joe Short. For six weeks their trap in Croucher's Bight overflowed with cod. With every haul after filling their own boats they hoisted flags as a signal for other fishermen to pull in and load up as well. It was the same everywhere on the Island that summer. While few families were prosperous all were comfortable.

The following summer of 1914, however, was a lean one for the cod fishery around Long Island and indeed in the whole northern half of Notre Dame Bay. Levi signed on with Robert Slade whose schooner, the Rose of Sharon was being outfitted for the Grey Islands, off the northeast coast of the Great Northern Peninsula. As a favoured location for the inshore fishing fleet from harbours all along the coast from Carbonear to Englee, Grey Islands Harbour was filled with schooners. The waters were teeming with great schools of cod. The crews worked from daylight to dark hauling the overflowing cod traps, splitting the fish and salting it down in the hole. There was barely time to think of home and family, let alone distractions in the outside world.

Oh, we don't want to lose you, But we think you ought to go
For your King and Your Country both need you so.
We shall want you and miss you but with all our might and
main
We will thank you, cheer you, kiss you,
When you come home again.

(Recruiting song from WW1)

WORD reached the Grey Islands in late July of 1914 that war clouds were gathering in Europe. The Archduke of Austria, Franz Ferdinand and his wife had been assassinated in a place called Sarajevo, Bosnia. Austria blamed Serbia and was intent on restoring its honor by force. Russia was mobilizing its forces as a warning to Austria. Kaiser Wilhelm of Germany was mobilizing the might of the German Armies to support his allies in Austria and to counter the threat from Russia. Britain and France were taking similar steps.

The ominous news reached the crew by telegraph in mid-August that a world war had indeed broken out and German forces were invading neutral Belgium and heading towards Paris. Governor Davidson in St. John's sent word to all communities that the entire British Empire was now at war with Germany. This sadly included Newfoundland. There was talk that it would be the worst war the world had ever known but most thought it would be over by Christmas.

The Rose of Sharon arrived back in Lush's Bight in late September. The fall harvest was in full swing as families filled their root cellars with potatoes, cabbage, turnip and other vegetables for the coming winter. Nonetheless, people were uneasy and fearful.

Governor Davidson's proclamation was prominently displayed in stores, the post office, and the Orange Lodge:

*The Mother Country has been compelled to go to war to pre-
serve...the rights and liberties which we all enjoy as citizens
of the British Empire...Newfoundland...has pledged to assist the Mother Country...a regiment of 500 men for land
service abroad...It is our duty and privilege, as loyal and
patriotic citizens of the empire to voluntarily assist....*

Public meetings brought together A Long Island Patriotic Committee. Members included George and Sam Paddock from Wards Harbour, Peter Brooks and Job Parsons
from Lush's Bight, Ken Short and Rueben Croucher from
Cutwell Harbour, John Rideout from the Arm. All were
only several generations removed from the old country
and all were determined to do their part for King George
and to bring Kaiser Bill to his knees.

A women's patriotic committee was given the task of
fundraising. With generous donations from merchants,
gifts of fish from fishermen and cash from socials more
than $200 had been raised by the end of December.

Levi's thoughts were elsewhere for much of the winter
of 1915. Miss Reid, a teacher from Trinity Bay had arrived
in The Harbour in September and was also boarding at the
Short's. She liked this serious young man and his adventurous spirit. He liked her sophistication and charm. Within a
few months they were making plans for the future.

They selected a site for their future home in a tiny
cove at the entrance to Cutwell Arm. It would be a modest
dwelling in a grassy meadow, with curving hills sheltering them from the north easterlies of winter. By Spring
Levi had cut enough logs for the timbers and boards that
would be needed to enclose the dwelling. He needed one
more fishing season to purchase the cement needed for a
foundation.

Throughout the winter the Patriotic Committee met
once a month to share news about the war. A magistrate
from Grand Falls was dispatched to the Island to recruit

young men but despite a strong turnout and a rousing speech there were no volunteers.

Men were planning for the summer fishery and surely the war would be over within the year as the great British Empire brought its might to bear. There were ominous signs that this would not be the case. In January the Germans had used zeppelins to bomb several British cities; there was a standoff in Europe; German submarines had sunk the great passenger liner, Lusitania, with horrendous loss of life.

Levi rejoined the crew of the Rose of Sharon for another summer at the Grey Islands in July of 1915 and as fate would dictate it would be his last. Many skippers along the coast that summer hired on youngsters no more than ten years old to replace older men who had left to join the 1st. Newfoundland Regiment.

Levi's friends, Nathaniel Croucher, Andrew Caravan, and Dolph Heath were the first to join up. Most of Levi's friends knew they would be expected to answer the call before long. Still, it was a good fishing season once again and after unloading the fish in Little Bay Islands each one of Bob Slade's crew was on good account with the Strong and Murcell merchants.

Levi completed the concrete foundation and the outside of his house before the first snowfalls of November brought a halt to the project. The young couple, who were now dreaming of a life together, knew the war would interrupt their plans.

At the last meeting of the Long Island Patriotic Committee in early December the minister, Rev. Howell, read a story from The Sun about the capture of a German soldier who had been found with a baby's hand in his pocket to take back as a souvenir to Germany...*just imagine, the devil must be in them...German barbarism...*

There was no doubt in anyone's mind where his duty lay. Many young men came forward at that meeting to volunteer, the Burtons, Willis, Sam, and Andrew; the Heath brothers; the Parsons boys from Lush's Bight, Andrew, Sid, and Alwin; Victor Colbourne and Joseph Paddock. Some were underage and would have to wait, others were held back by anxious parents but over the next year twenty-three young men had enlisted. Levi wrote his name in a tentative script on the enlistment form.

He reported to the medical officer of the First Newfoundland Regiment at Pleasantville, St. John's on a mild Tuesday morning, the 4th of April 1916. He was weighed, measured and probed, declared to be 5 feet 6 inches tall, 122 pounds with a 36 inch chest. The scar on his cheek, a souvenir of the coal mines, was duly noted and he was declared medically fit.

His enlistment papers indicated that sixty cents per day was to be deposited to the Bank of Montreal until a debt of forty dollars was paid to Strong and Murcell at Little Bay Islands. After the debt was settled the same amount was to be deposited to an account in the name of his sister, Mrs. Andrew Hewlett, living at Cutwell Harbour, Long Island.

Three months of basic military training followed with a 5:30 AM wake-up, breakfast at 6:00 AM, one hour of physical exercise beginning at 7:00, then parade ground drills with rifles until noon. They drilled and drilled and then drilled some more until each company moved as one through the early morning fogs of the St. John's spring.

They endured long route marches, at first to Mundy Pond and soon along the dirt roads to Logy Bay and Outer Cove. Rifle practice and skirmishes along the barren South Side Hills brought out curious children who watched as their heroes prepared for battle. For ten long weeks they learned the basics of soldiering. When rumours circulated about a great July Drive which would push the enemy back into Germany, they grew uneasy about missing the action. Then came the stories about the battle of Beaumont Hamel. The disaster destroyed their youthful innocence and brought home the horrors of war.

The accounts of the tragedy dominated the headlines in the St. John's papers. On July 1st near the small village of Beaumont Hamel, 800 young men of the First Newfoundland Regiment moved off at 9:15 through an early morning mist and into the face of murderous machine gun fire. Forty-five minutes later barely 70 remained standing. The regiment had been annihilated.

Somewhere on the stretch of no-man's land in front of Beaumont Hamel lay the body of Levi's friend, Nathaniel Croucher, from Cutwell Arm. He was barely twenty years old.

On July 18th, "A" and "B' Companies of the 3rd Battalion of the Newfoundland Regiment formed up at Pleasantville for inspection by His Excellency, Governor Davidson, and Prime Minister Morris. The governor lauded the troops as 'being exceptionally high in physique, character, and aptitude for war." Next day the 500 soldiers embarked for the UK on the SS Scicilian.

Old photographs of their departure show the soldiers perched precariously in the riggings and crowding the decks to catch a last look at their homeland as the ship cleared the Narrows and met the heavy swells of the open North Atlantic. It was an uneventful crossing of eleven days on a crowded ship to the British naval base at Devenport. There they boarded an overnight train to the regiment's training depot at Ayr on the west coast of Scotland.

The three months of basic training in the familiar confines of St. John's left Levi and his comrades ill prepared for the tough training regime now imposed on them.

Battle hardened veterans of the regiment's Gallipoli campaign as well as expert British instructors molded the
unit into a fighting force. Sixteen hour days were filled
with gruelling physical training, bayonet fighting, trench
digging, and overland skirmishes.

Despite the punishing schedule, there was time for
Levi and his friends to revel in several short leaves into
Ayr, to enjoy meals with Scottish families and attend
dances with local girls. Occasionally they overindulged at
the village pub on the High Street. But these were momentary lapses of discipline prior to facing the harsh reality of the trenches.

"A" and "B" Companies made their farewell march
through the friendly streets of Ayr in early October as
autumn colors were settling over the Scottish hills. Their
goal now was to provide a speedy reinforcement for their
much depleted regiment at the front. Ten days of 'battle
school' awaited them at Rouen just across the channel
in France. The young men scrambled beneath barbed
wire barriers under live fire, practised trench raiding and
hand to hand combat. They listened intently to the instructions of those who had already been through the hell
of the Somme.

On his birthday, October 14, Levi and his company
joined the Newfoundland Regiment in the field. He was
twenty-six years old. Their camp was just a few miles
from the small French city of Albert and not far from
Beaumont Hamel. Their march through the sucking mud
of the Somme front was a fitting initiation to the punishing conditions of the trenches.

The late fall weather had now worsened with continuous cold rain during the day and frost at night. Before the
month was out bitter northeast winds and snow envel-
oped the surrounding countryside in a curtain of misery.

Enemy shelling was a constant disruption to fitful sleep. Stagnant water overflowed the duckboards at the bottom of the trenches. Many of Levi's fellow soldiers came down with trench foot, a painful condition brought on by the dampness. Blisters, swelling and open sores covered feet and ankles. Untreated it led to gangrene and amputation. The simple solution was to keep the feet dry, a near impossible challenge in the sea of mud.

Adding to their misery were the rats, an infestation of millions, feeding on the unrecovered dead in no-man's land and scurrying through the dugouts searching for the men's rations. Conditions were so bad that officers were forced to rotate their troops in and out of the trenches every three to four days.

For the soldiers there was a silver lining in the dark clouds hovering low over the battlefield. The long interval of foul winter weather meant the end of allied offensive action which had begun with the Great July Drive. The slaughter would subside.

In the four short months since July 1st the allies had suffered 600,000 casualties, the Germans, another 450,000. The First Newfoundland Regiment itself had suffered worse than any other comparable unit in the British Expeditionary Force.

In early December the regiment was taken out of the line altogether. Those few with at least six months service in the trenches were allowed furlough in England and the remainder sent back to a rest area in the small French village of Camps-en-Amienois. They were to spend a month amongst simple rural farm families who knew nothing about those strangers from across the sea.

The official history of the regiment notes that "as the battalion swung down the poplar lined road the villagers watched with expressions which suggested that they feared the worst. The cheerful smiles of the newcomers soon seemed to reassure them, however, and within a few hours the Newfoundlanders were quite at home, drinking cafe-au-lait in the kitchens of various village homes."

Christmas was celebrated with mail and gifts from home, tobacco, cookies, and warm wool socks. Most welcome of all was a substantial shipment of salt cod and hard bread. To everyone's chagrin there was no salt pork. In a moment of inspiration while searching the local butcher shops one of the Newfoundland cooks spotted 'lardon', a fine French bacon. Those who first turned up their noses soon discovered fish and brewis with a much richer flavour.

The young men from Newfoundland celebrated Christmas service with the rest of the villagers at the fourteenth century stone chapel in the town square. As the chaplain recounted the timeless story of birth and rebirth, Levi's thoughts were of a home in a sheltered cove at the mouth of Cutwell Arm. But his family was thousands of miles away and peace on earth, remained a fleeting dream. His regiment began its move back to the front on January 11, 1917.

Levi's spirits were lifted when a good friend, Edgar Blackmore from Pilley's Island, unexpectedly reported for duty with the regiment in the field. Edgar had signed on a year earlier but had been posted on various assignments in Ayr since then. For the next two months the pair saw continuous action in the trenches as the regiment followed up on strategies to keep the enemy off balance.

The frosty weather created a quagmire both in and out of the trenches. Soldiers slipping off the duckboards found themselves up to their waist in the sticky mud. The limited offensive action did not eliminate casualties entirely. Constant shelling and trench raids by the Germans resulted in losses of 27 killed and 44 wounded by March 3 when the regiment was taken out of the line and sent back to Camps-en- Amienois for a rest period.

The townspeople talked about an old-fashioned winter, and it proved to be a classic farmer's understatement. Temperatures from the end of December to the end of March were bitterly cold. Biting winds blew in from the far north bringing blizzards and heavy snow to many parts of Europe. Back home in Newfoundland this was winter as usual and for young men from the northeast coast it was nothing to complain about. For the warlords on both sides, the bad weather provided a let-up to plan new strategies for breaking the stalemate.

Despite heavy losses, General Haig now planned a great push centered on the city of Arras. It was underneath this old city that the British had discovered a vast network of tunnels burrowed into the underlying chalk. These tunnels could be extended out into no-man's land and used to bring soldiers closer to the enemy lines.

Above ground the offensive would begin with "the greatest artillery bombardment the world had ever seen." Coupled with the massed artillery, the big guns would deliver poison gas shells into the German lines to add additional death, destruction and terror. A new weapon, the tank, would be added for good measure.

It all came with a promise of victory within 48 hours. The German forces suspected the big push was coming and began a quiet retreat to better positions on the Hindenburg line. At the same time they perfected the "elastic defense," a tactic they were to use with devastating effect against the Newfoundlanders a month later.

The great offensive, now known as the Battle of Arras, was launched against the enemy lines in the early morning hours of April 9th, Easter Monday, 1917. With a biting easterly wind driving snow and sleet into their faces, British and colonial troops caught the enemy forces off balance and achieved significant success.

The Canadians captured Vimy Ridge, a formidable objective that had eluded capture by British and French forces for two years. At the end of the first day thousands of enemy soldiers were prisoners. The allied forces had pushed several miles into German lines. By the next day, however, the Germans began to recover and by day three were able to plug the gaps in their lines.

On the 12th Levi and his fellow Newfoundlanders moved up the line towards the sound of the big guns. They established their headquarters in the centre of Monchy, a village at the easterly edge of a bulge in the German lines. In tactical terms it was like a long balloon extending into enemy defences. Some junior officers questioned the wisdom of extending the balloon further and leaving themselves dangerously exposed on both flanks. The mission of the Newfoundlanders, along with their sister regiment, the Essex on their left, was to capture the high ground fifteen hundred yards in front of the town.

Zero hour was 5:30 a.m. April 14th. It was quiet and cold. Just before dawn Levi Normore, Elijah Blackmore, Lance Corporal Beaton Colbourne, and a thousand others from both regiments readied themselves to go over the top.

In the grey mist of that early Saturday morning they could barely make out their main objective, Infantry Hill. A secondary objective, a neck of woods known as the Bois du Vert was visible on their right. Their sister regiment the 1st Essex was preparing to advance on their left.

A few Germans soldiers could be clearly seen leaving their dugouts and running back from their front line. For the first several hundred yards the Newfoundlanders cautiously advanced and ran into weak resistance. They found enemy trenches abandoned and were now confident of an easy victory.

Capt. Leo C. Murphy, a regimental historian, writing in 1937, described what happened next through an eye-witness account: *"They were waiting for us...truly it might be said that we ran into it. The pat-pat-pat of the machine guns is regular and intensive. You feel the wood is filled with Germans. Men are falling right and left... We are being peppered, and you have lost Richards and Colbourne...it is getting warm. Field-grey uniforms coming down in open formation...The Essex breaking up on the left. Your platoon sergeant is dead by your side...Fred Janes, of the Red Cross, comes out and tries to dress your wound. Something hits him between the shoulders..."*

The Essex and the Newfoundland battalions had walked into a trap. Those that tried to get back to Monchy were shot down in the murderous fire coming from both sides. Levi Normore and his friend from Pilley's Island died somewhere in the confusion of the advance and the retreat. Their bodies were never recovered.

The wounded, in their hundreds, lay screaming in the shell holes only to be killed later by their own artillery. Those that survived were taken prisoner. By noon it was over, the two battalions had ceased to exist. The Newfoundland Regiment had lost 17 officers and 468 men of other ranks, the Essex, 17 officers and 585 men of other ranks.

For the second time in eight months the Newfoundland regiment was eliminated as a fighting force. The senseless disaster sparked a minor revolt amongst staff officers in the British Expeditionary Force and a report to the General Staff complained of futile losses without adequate gain.

DINAH Normore, Levi's adoptive mother, received the ominous news on May 13 that her son was missing in action as a result of the battle in early April. Rumours circulated on the Island that he was a prisoner of war in Germany. Others believed that he was gravely wounded and lying in a French hospital.

It would take the British Records office in London another six months to confirm with the German Government that he was not a prisoner of war and at the end of October the cable from the Colonial Office in St. John's confirmed that he was presumed dead. Final documents, including details of his estate, did not arrive in Newfoundland until the end of May, 1918.

These personal papers were to spark another conflict on Long Island between Annie Eliza, the birth mother, and the Normores, who were the adoptive family. The paymaster of the Newfoundland Regiment confirmed that Bertha was the designated beneficiary for the bank account at the Bank of Montreal. This piece of news did not take long to circulate around the Island.

When Annie Eliza learned of the arrangements for Levi's estate she wrote a detailed letter to Lieut. Col. Rendell, chief staff officer of the regiment, outlining the circumstances of Levi's birth, baptism and subsequent adoption in a tone of anguish for a lost child and bitterness towards those who had chosen him to be their son:

> *...just think is it not worth a thought for one to loose (sic) my son and all he has, and then to see strangers enjoying my poor boy's goods. Any parent in a sane state would see the wrong in it. Hoping that you will try and do all that you can for me to obtain my rights of my son's money and property...*

On August 28th, 1918, Annie Eliza received a response from Lieut. Col. Rendell:

Dear Madam:
...When No. 2425, Private Levi Normore enlisted, he gave
Mrs. Dinah Normore as his mother and next of kin. The
report that Private Normore was missing on April 14, 1917
was notified to her on May 13th, 1917, and a later report
that he was believed killed in action on April 14 was sent
to her on Nov. 7th. This soldier's estate is now in the hands
of the Minister of Justice awaiting administration papers.
The estate is, as far as is at present known, to be adminis-
tered to Mrs. Dinah Normore. No personal effects of this sol-
dier have yet been received, but when they have eventually
come to hand, they will be sent to Mrs. Dinah Normore...

Lieut. Col Rendell, perhaps hoping to avoid a conflict
over a fallen soldier's personal effects, tactfully left the
door open for Annie to pursue the matter further. She
could send him a declaration signed by a justice of the
peace or magistrate.

The two competing claims would then be referred
to the Department of Justice. On the 9th of November,
just two days before peace was declared in Europe, Annie swore an oath before K. K. Short, J. P. that she was
indeed the natural mother of Private Levi Normore. The
Department of Justice, ignoring the documented wishes
of the dead soldier, subsequently ruled in Annie Eliza's
favour and on May 30, 1919 the Department of Militia
complied with the ruling:

Mrs. James Colbourne
Lush's Bight.
Dear Madam
I enclose cheque for $66.98, balance of estate of late Pte. L
Normore, due you as administratix of his estate.
JMS Howley (Paymaster)

Dinah Normore, a widow now eighty years old, moved

to Pilleys Island in 1919 to live with her daughter. She was now destitute and forced to live on a poor allowance of $7 per quarter. With the assistance of the Salvation Army she made several claims for a separation allowance in 1919 and 1920 citing the loss of her son, Levi, who had been her only support. Typical of the responses she received from the Department of Militia was the following:

April 15, 1920
Mrs. Dinah Normore, Pilley's Island, N.D.B.
Dear Madam:
With reference to your application for Separation Allowance, I have been directed to state that the same cannot be granted to you, because your dependence on your son Levi is not shown in view of the fact that he did not make any allotment to you.
Yours truly,

In 1923, the Government of Newfoundland presented Dinah with a Memorial Plaque as next of kin to a soldier killed in the Great War. She also received a photo of Levi, posing proudly in his Royal Newfoundland Regiment uniform. Her son, George, tried unsuccessfully to have the regiment provide funding for a monument to his lost brother.

In her grief, Bertha was determined that Levi would not be forgotten and some years later after much sacrifice and effort she purchased a small monument to her beloved brother. It was erected in a quiet cemetery midway between the villages of Wards Harbour and Quenton's Cove. The simple inscription on the headstone reads, "IN LOVING MEMORY OF NUMBER 2425, LEVI NORMORE, KILLED IN ACTION AT MONCHY LE PREUX, FRANCE, APRIL 14TH 1917. HE GAVE HIS LIFE FOR HIS FRIENDS."

Levi's dream home which he had painstakingly built near the mouth of Cutwell Arm stood silently for decades as a prominent symbol of the young man's sacrifice. Eventually its walls caved in. White birch, alder and wild raspberry took over the small meadow and the site of the house itself. Levi's cement foundation poured in 1915 has stood the test of time and is still clearly visible in the undergrowth.

From the east comes the low rumble of the ocean waves washing on the headlands.

DISAPPEARED

...They looked for me in the cafes, cemeteries and churches
but they did not find me
They never found me?
No, they never found me

Federco Garcia Lorca,
Fable and Round of the Three Friends

"TRY to find Uncle Eric," were Amelia's parting words to one of her sons as he was leaving to attend university in England in 1975. It was a profound indication that she had not given up hope, after fifty painful years, that the brother she idolized as a child would one day turn up and walk in the door as if he had been gone for only a few months. She was just seven years old when Eric left home, and disappeared forever, in that fateful spring of 1925. He was seventeen years old.

Despite having a large family of her own, her lost brother was never far from her thoughts. Often, as her children were growing up in the busy household, she appeared lost in the deep silences that came with regular bouts of depression over his disappearance. These periods always ended with "I wonder what happened to Eric." She mulled over all the possibilities. At times she felt strongly that he had been murdered but could offer no evidence that this had happened. At other times she was convinced he had been killed during the war after joining the armed forces of either, Canada, Great Britain or the United States but there was no evidence of that either. A comprehensive search of the military records of each country in recent years came up empty.

Sometimes, too, there was a simpler explanation, closer to home. Down through the years there was much speculation on the Island that he may have walked into the danger area at the mouth of Long Tickle where every year the rip tides weakened the winter sea ice covering the bay. According to this theory Eric would have fallen through the ice and drowned somewhere between the island and the mainland on the day he left the community in the spring of 1925.

Eric was born in February, 1908, the first of fifteen children for Bessie and Samuel (Sammy) Ledrew. By February of 1919 when Amelia was born, three of the children Bramwell, Dulcie and Annie, had died of whooping cough, or influenza. Another child, Julie, succumbed to pneumonia in 1921 and Lily, the last child, born in 1933, died in infancy that same year of an unknown illness. There were no doctors and no miracle drugs. Death was a constant companion to the Ledrew family.

The grieving parents put the tragedies behind them and focused instead on raising the surviving children; Josh, born in 1910; Robert in 1914; Mabel in 1916; Amelia in 1919; Selby, Ralph, Otto and Phyllis, born in the 1920's; and the youngest daughter Ruby in 1931. All were, at one time or another, obsessed with locating their brother.

Unlike most people on the island, Sammy had no family history in the fishery. When he married Bessie Raines in December of 1907 he was working for the Anglo Newfoundland Development (AND) Company on the construction of a paper mill at Grand Falls on the Exploits

River. Had he been selected as one of the new employees in the mill when it opened in 1909 he would certainly have moved to the booming industrial centre in the interior of Newfoundland with its new hospital and school, and life would have turned out differently. But it was a closed company town, and without a permanent job in the mill he was refused entry.

In the years to follow, Sammy and several of his sons made a living cutting timber for the paper company. Low wages and deplorable conditions in the camps made life difficult. Woodcutters lived on a diet of beans and hard bread and spent their nights picking body lice from their undershirts. Sammy was fond of saying, "I made cash money and I suffered for it." The cash gave the family independence on an island where merchants ruled the roost and most people saw no real money in their whole lifetime.

Down through the years, rumours persisted that Eric had differences with his father and they parted on bitter terms. It is impossible to know whether the rumours had any basis in fact or were simply the gossip of a small town. Most certainly the younger man was adventurous and wanted a different life away from the

Sammy and Bessie Ledrew, 1953. Twenty-Eight Years after their Son's Disappearance

Island and away from the back-breaking work of the lumber camps. Most of his brothers and sisters were similarly inclined and by 1950 all but one, Nellie, had departed for greener pastures in far off Canada or to more urban area on the Island of Newfoundland.

Correspondence from Ruby, who moved to Toronto in the late 1940's and made a career in the banking industry, would place the rumour of family conflict in considerable doubt. She maintains that there was some correspondence between Eric and his mother and father for a couple of years after he left and they always expected that he would return.

The letters home were postmarked from the Seamen's Church Institute (SCI) in New York. The institute was a safe haven for mariners in a city where they were otherwise easy prey for 'the crimps', a criminal gang which targeted foreign seamen. The SCI offered rooms, meals, entertainment, post office and banking services, as well as spiritual guidance for its guests. The building at 25 South Street, on the waterfront in New York, became so popular that it was expanded in 1926 as thousands of seamen made it their home while in port.

In 2008, Ruby also voiced one of the puzzling mysteries of her brother's disappearance, "The last letter my mom received from Eric stated that he was going someplace where he would not be able to write her for about five years. Mom never heard from him again." Unfortunately no one remembered when the letter was written.

Robert, who was eleven years old when his brother left, drew his own conclusions from this last letter and stated on many occasions that Eric was engaged as a crew member on a rum runner. It was a logical explanation although others in the family disputed the assumption.

In 1919 the United States Congress passed the Volstead Act, better known as the National Prohibition Law which banned the selling and transport of intoxicating beverages throughout the US. It remained in force until 1933. The

The Seamen's Church Institute, on the waterfront, New York, circa 1925. Photo Courtesy of SCI Archives.

new law created an interesting paradox where drinking was still perfectly legal, however, no one could purchase or sell alcoholic beverages. The result was a massive upsurge of criminal activity as lawless gangs and shrewd individuals cashed in on the business of satisfying the cravings of a thirsty population. The centre of the activity was along the US east coast. Savvy skippers loaded their ships with rum in the Bahamas, Canadian whiskey in Montreal, as well as wines and brandies in St. Pierre. Their task was to outwit the American Coast Guard and deliver the goods to their customers all along the US east coast.

Those who were caught received lenient treatment from sympathetic juries and of the first 4000 cases to come before New York courts only five were found guilty and just one received a short prison sentence. The most famous of the rum runners, a skipper named William S. McCoy, received only a nine month sentence and was allowed to keep the small fortune he had amassed in the business.

The public, and the juries convened by the courts, saw rum runners and bootleggers in general as 'honest law-breakers', making it unlikely that Eric would have received a five year sentence had he been involved in the illegal trade in booze.

One of the most disturbing incidents with respect to Eric's disappearance happened at Tommy's Arm, Newfoundland after the Second World War. At the time, Tommy's Arm, in central Notre Dame Bay was a transhipment port for pulpwood exports to Scandinavian and European countries. The arrival of overseas freighters with large crews was a common occurrence during the summer months. Often these foreign crew members would come ashore to trade liquor and other goods for items not readily available on board their ships.

On one particular occasion, so the story goes, a strange sailor disembarked from a Swedish ship and began inquiring about the Ledrew family, mentioning specifically Sammy and Bessie as well as some of their sons. The stranger was privy to details which could only be known to a member of the family. The rumour gained traction and quickly reached Eric's mother and father on the Island. Filled with anxiety and anticipation, Sammy and Bessie made their way to Tommy's Arm by motor boat to investigate. Unfortunately their hopes were turned to hurt and disappointment and the reports were unfounded. We now know that it was one variation of a common urban legend in which a long lost person appears seeking information on his family and then just as mysteriously vanishes again. At best it was a cruel joke.

The youngest Ledrew brother, Otto, born in 1926, began his own search for his lost brother in the 1960's.

At the time he was working in New York and decided to check out the Seamen's Institute. This effort, too, led to a dead end, as the original building had been demolished and the SCI had moved to a new location.

More recent searches for clues to Eric's disappearance have led to similar dead ends. Typical was an entry in Canadian Immigration Records for 1928 which noted passengers arriving at North Sydney, Nova Scotia on the gulf ferry, the Kyle. At this time, of course, Newfoundland and Canada were separate dominions. The record shows: Eric Ledrew, approximate date of birth: 1911; Date of Arrival: 31 May 1928; Port of Departure: Port Aux Basques, Newfoundland. On the surface, given that only an approximate date of birth is recorded, this appeared to be the right person. A more detailed analysis of the records, however, revealed that this Eric Ledrew was born at Cupids, Newfoundland, and was travelling to join his father who was working in Montreal.

There was also the distinct possibility that Eric's name would appear in some of the archival holdings of the Seamen's Church Institute at its new location in New York. These holdings include a large collection of photographs, scrapbooks, and minutes of board meetings. A search of these documents by the assistant archivist turned up nothing. Unfortunately, the registers of the SCI in which all sailor's names were recorded, have not survived.

The first and only piece of solid evidence indicating Eric's trail is contained in a document from the Port Authority of New York dated March 3, 1927. On this date a three masted sailing ship, the Esther Adelaide, docked in New York harbour. The vessel, better known as a tern schooner, was the work horse of the day, carrying heavy cargoes of timber, coal and gypsum from Canada to the United States along the east coast of North America. Because of their design the tern schooners were highly manoeuvrable in coastal waters and typically carried small crews of six or seven men.

The ship's manifest supplied to the US Customs Service is now available from the National Archives in Washington, D.C. It provides a list of seven crew members on the Esther Adelaide: the skipper, Joseph C. Merriam; mate, George Marwick, cook and steward, Eric Ledrew; deckhands, Hayward Parsons, Edward Shepard, David Malloy, and Abram Marshall. Eric is listed as nineteen years of age, five feet eight and one half inches tall and 152 pounds. Crewmembers, Ledrew, Parsons, Shepard and Malloy are all noted as young sailors from Newfoundland. The information provides a precise match for the missing brother and son.

The Esther Adelaide sailed from New York on its return voyage to Halifax April 23, 1927. Before departure the skipper, Joseph C. Merriam, filed a statement with US Customs indicating that one of the crew, Hayward Parsons, had deserted the ship.

Eric returned to Halifax on the Esther Adelaide in April of 1927. Whether he stayed with the ship is an open question which can only be answered by a detailed study of port records. The schooner itself continued in the usual shipping trades between Canada and the US until 1934 when she was abandoned on the beach at Parrsboro, Nova Scotia. In 1936 she was bought, reconditioned, renamed the Cinalta and put back in the usual trades. The old workhorse sank without loss of life in Long Island Sound on May 3, 1942.

Sammy and Bessie died in the early 1970s without any answers to the questions surrounding their son's disappearance.

POSTSCRIPT

"Mother" Janet Roper worked at the Seamen's Church Institute from 1915 to 1943. Originally hired as house mother she is best known for establishing the Missing Seamen's Bureau formed in response to requests from families all over the world for help in locating their missing sons. The searches took anywhere from a few hours to several years and occurred mainly by word of mouth. Had the Ledrew family been aware of her work at the time she may well have located Eric.

BANNERMAN OF THE DANDENONG

The whining schoolboy, with his satchel
And his shining morning face, creeping snail like
Unwillingly to school.

William Shakespeare, AS YOU LIKE IT, Act II, Scene VII

THE new teacher had not yet replaced the prominent picture of King George hanging above the blackboard. The newly arrived portrait of a faintly smiling Queen Elizabeth gathered dust underneath the big hardwood desk. The old king's eyes appeared to be always moving so that no matter where you were in the school room his stern gaze followed. He wore a permanent frown that filled the classroom as if reminding the lesser mortals beneath his stare that he was aware of their every misdeed and impure thought. The teacher believed in biblical discipline and his demeanour matched that of the king.

The twenty restless scholars tried to adjust to the new teacher's iron rule. They fidgeted in silence, averting their eyes from the list of common sins. Those sins were prominently written in large aggressive words on the right side of the chalkboard which lined the front wall of the school room. On the left side was a corresponding list of punishments for those tempted to stray from the straight and narrow: Writing Notes – Four Strokes of the Strap; Lateness – Five Strokes; Smoking – Six Strokes; Talking in

Class – Standing in the Corner; Slenging – Ten strokes.

Freddie reasoned that if he didn't read the rules he could hardly be accused of breaking them. Hadn't Uncle Andrew mentioned something about nine tenths of the law. His momentary attempt to avoid reality was interrupted by the teacher.

"Now, Freddie," intoned Mr. Whitson, "Can you explain to everyone what a slenger is?"

"It means, sir, you have to do your work and not be slenging around," answered Freddie in a guilt tinged voice.

Freddie, a grade seven senior, was a spirited student with a bent for getting into trouble. He found it difficult to sit quietly at work for long periods of time and was often caught in the act of creatively communicating with those around him. Sometimes he used notes in code and sent them by paper airplane when the teacher's back was turned. To complicate matters both he and Howie, his classmate, were smitten by Ruby, the dark haired girl in grade seven. Freddie rarely completed his assigned homework, always claiming he had so much to do at home that he did not have the time. When Mr. Whitson needed a trigger for his many eruptions of bad temper, he did not have far to look.

One rainy morning in October the students were given the option of staying in class for recess. None did, since being outside, getting wet, was preferable to the oppression of the school house. Freddie convinced five of the older boys and the girls to participate in a game of corners in the unlit porch leading to the deck. The rules of the game were rather loose but everyone knew that the real goal was to have a boy and a girl occupy the same corner at the same time, like a combination of tag and musical chairs in the dark.

Shocking Conditions in Small Schools: a motion to ask the Department of Education to investigate conditions – described as "shocking" in small schools in isolated areas, particularly along the Northern peninsula...at Saturday night's session of the Newfoundland Teacher's Association...A letter was read outlining the situation in Northern outports including the Green Bay area. The letter told of one and two room schools staffed by inadequately trained teachers many of whom had not passed grade X themselves.

(*Twillingate Sun*, August 16, 1952)

As with all juvenile games, spontaneity overcame common sense and the noise level increased as students collided and grabbed each other in the blackness trying to avoid being tagged. It must have disturbed Mr. Whitson. The inside door suddenly flew open revealing a face contorted with rage. Each of the boys was taken by the collar and flung into a growing heap of tangled arms and legs on the classroom floor.

When class resumed the boys found themselves standing in front of the large wooden desk awaiting further punishment. Under intense questioning it was established that Freddie was the ring leader of 'the racket in the porch' as Mr. Whitson called it. Poor Freddie was sentenced to receive ten strokes of the strap while the others, except the girls, were to get five. Each girl was sent to stand in a corner of the classroom for half an hour balancing a book on her head. Later there was some debate about whether this was a less painful form of punishment.

Mr. Whitson pulled the dreaded leather strap from his desk drawer and ordered Freddie to stretch his hands in front of him. With heavy measured strokes the leather bit into the fleshy part of his outstretched hand near the wrist. It dug into the palm, and extended its burning pain along the fingertips. Like a striking snake the head of the instrument wrapped partially around the back of his hand.

Each blow resounded with a sharp 'thwack' around the quiet class. Each child in the room winced as the blow was struck.

Towards the end Freddie was standing on his toes, his face contorted in pain. Tears appeared in the corners of his eyes and ran down the side of his face. Everyone noticed the strange mixture of rage and pleasure on the teacher's face. The other boys in the line were reduced to quivering flesh. They all said afterwards that the sound of the leather hitting bare hands was harder on the nerves than the strap itself.

The incident took its emotional toll on the students and a heavy quiet settled on the room for the rest of the day. Freddie did not return to school next morning. His mother tried to reduce the swelling in his hands by soaking them in salty water.

She complained to Rue, the school board chairman that the teacher's punishment of the children had gone a bit overboard and wondered whether Mr. Whitson's strap was regulation. "Perhaps you ought to measure it," she suggested, "and perhaps while you're at it you ought to ask the teacher why he had to leave the last place he was in."

EDUCATION: Within a few days school will begin for another term. Pencils and textbooks will soon be in use again. That early morning scramble to find missing homework and windbreakers will start once again. Summer holidays, that much longed for time in June, will be ended and many will be returning to school ... Others will want to go back while others will be going for the first time. There will be a real thrill for these small children...

(Twillingate Sun, August 30, 1952)

MR. Whitson had arrived on the island in the dead of night, on the very day before the long summer holiday ended, so there was no time to take the measure of the man. An early September nor'easter was doing its best to delay the inevitable school opening. On approaching the harbour late Sunday afternoon, the captain of the MV Codroy, the coastal steamer, had decided to anchor in the shelter of Oil Island rather than risk getting too close to the shoal at the entrance to the harbour. Sometime after midnight a motor launch delivered its wet cargo and a thoroughly drenched teacher to the government wharf. Rue met him there and introduced himself as chairman of the school board.

"You may be the chairman, sir," responded the teacher, "but I am in charge here."

Rue ignored the remark but felt a twinge of misgiving about the man in front of him. He duly escorted Mr. Whitson to Vi's boarding house.

Aunt Vi, as everyone called her, had met all shapes and sizes in her day but this new one made her a little uneasy. Mr. Whitson was no sooner welcomed into the household when he made it clear that this was not his preferred community. He had hoped to stay in Muddy Hole but through some mix up the board there had assumed he had resigned. They had gone ahead and hired a replacement teacher without his knowledge. "A bad lot," He called them "with no gratitude for straightening out their brats." Aunt Vi later observed, in her colourful manner of speaking, that the poor thing had a bitter sort of look on his face like he had been sucking on green apples. Looking back everyone should have seen all of this as a bad omen.

The community was seen as a sleepy backwater and a little too isolated to attract the best and the brightest. The people were simple fisher folk, independent and proud. They readily trusted the teacher and the clergy to provide earthly knowledge and spiritual guidance to their children. This year the local school board had searched all summer long for a new teacher. The previous one had decided to accept a better position in Grand Falls. Then in late August, frantic telegrams were sent to the government offices in St. John's begging for assistance to keep the one room school open.

At the last minute, one teacher was left over after all the other schools on the northeast coast were ready for classes. Thus the community was blessed with the appointment of Mr. Whitson.

The school board chairman walked door to door with his solemn expression spreading the good news about the new teacher. Mothers were relieved and looked forward to a much needed breather after a long summer having all the youngsters underfoot.

"He was last year in Muddy Hole, very strict!" Rue announced, and then, nodding to the children with a chuckle in his voice and a twinkle in his eye, "He's already ordered a bigger strap than the last one."

This last statement was meant as a warning to the young ones as well as a reminder to grateful parents that sparing the rod was not the way to raise good Christian children.

On the first Monday morning in September most of the twenty eager scholars, with well-scrubbed faces showing a mixture of fear and anticipation, were lined up outside the one room school house. Freddie, Howie and several other boys had broken off from the group to lasso a goat that had the misfortune to wander by. Its bleating of distress were interrupted by a shouted warning from Betsy who had spotted the new teacher walking slowly along the shore road. The boys scrambled back to the line.

The girls primped in the sunny new dresses their mothers had bought from the old Jewish pedlar who showed up every August with his oversize suitcases. The boys were more ill at ease in their new plaid shirts and denim pants, an informal dress code made possible by Eaton's Fall Catalogue.

The older girls held the hands of tiny shivering primer children. The older boys tried to hide their worried faces as Mr. Whitson, showing the stress of his stormy arrival the previous night, made his way up the hill.

He was a small man with a slight limp, a pinched face and angry eyes. In one hand he held a bulging brown satchel. There was not a hint of greeting as the student body parted, allowing him up the steps and into the schoolhouse. The question as to whether the students should follow was answered with an emphatic bang of the door.

Momentarily he reappeared waving a clanging bell. The children streamed into the room, dividing naturally into small groups by age and grade. The older students gravitated to the larger desks along the window side overlooking the harbour.

An uneasy silence filled the air as Mr. Whitson introduced himself and proceeded to unload the contents of his satchel; some tattered books which were arranged neatly on a corner of the desk; a ticking alarm clock placed to face the class; and then, with a slow and deliberate gesture he reached into the bag and both hands emerged reverently holding an oversized leather strap, tapered at one end for grip, and custom designed to inflict maximum pain.

"I will call the roll," he announced in his high pitched teacher voice. "Each person will raise their hand when I call their name."

He started with the older students.

"Betsy,"

Betsy raised her hand in acknowledgement.

"Norma," "Wilmore," with a noticeable pause he studied each nervous face in turn, memorizing the features.

"Freddie."

"Here sir," said Freddie.

"I've told you just to raise your hand, Freddie, I don't want to hear your voice. How old are you?"

"Me, sir?" replied Freddie.

"Yes, you Sir! Who do you think I'm talking to, the man in the bloody moon? It says here that you're fourteen but you're only in grade seven. You're not very swift are you, Freddie."

Freddie lowered his head, knowing he had blundered into a trap. "No, sir," he mumbled. Mr. Whitson moved on.

"Howie."

"Here, sir," responded Howie, casually.

"Are you deaf and dumb, too, Howie?" There was now a distinct tone of menace in his voice. "I can just tell that you and Freddie are going to be great examples for the rest of the students, this year."

"Yes, sir," said Howie. There was a hint of defiance in the voice.

"Ruby," Shouted Mr. Whitson.

Just about all the students were registered when Little Millie could no longer contain her pent up tension. A pool of water formed underneath her tiny desk.

"What's the child's name?" demanded Mr. Whitson.

"Everybody calls her Little Millie," offered Betsy, helpfully, "but her real name is Millie Little." Betsy was about to offer additional information but was abruptly overruled.

"From now on she's to be called just 'Millie' in this school. If she's old enough to come to school she's got to

learn not to wet her clothes. Do you understand, Millie?"
The child whimpered in fear and abject shame.

"Betsy, you are to take the child home to her mother.
She can come back after recess," barked the teacher.

Howie and Freddie were ordered to clean up the mess.

THE grade seven students, now paired with Howie and
Freddie at the senior level, lost their privileged position
along the harbour window within the first month. Perhaps, Mr. Whitson noticed the undue attention being paid
to the older girls by their dreamy admirers as numerous
written messages were transmitted along the wall. Perhaps, too, he noticed the stolen glances and wistful looks
on the boys' faces at the sound of every fishing boat, with
its make and break motor, stuttering out to the fishing
grounds. Sometimes on the bright fall days of Indian
summer the calm stretch of ocean in the Run seemed to
float above itself lulling the boys into a trance like state.
At such times, Mr. Whitson developed the habit of creeping quietly along the aisle between the rows of desks and
with a deft flick of his wrist wrapped the strap around the
head of an unsuspecting offender.

The senior boys simply came to school one late October morning and found their desks moved against the opposite wall. The primer students who could not see out
the window in any case now occupied this coveted space.
Howie and Freddie, like two bookends, positioned at either end of the senior row, chafed at the new arrangements. To add insult to injury, the girls maintained a
semi privileged position in the next row to the window
but the social order was now upset and it became impossible for the boys to talk to the girls without being noticed.

Things started to come apart when Mr. Whitson assigned the senior class to learn his favourite poem, 'Bannerman of the Dandenong' over the weekend. By 'learn'

he meant 'memorize' and by 'memorize' he meant twelve long verses that the students could not get their heads around. It was an epic tale of two young men racing through the Australian outback ahead of a raging bush fire. One rode a slow grey horse and Bannerman, his friend, rode his swift bay mare. Each was on a journey to be reunited with the girl of his dreams. They soon realized they were meeting the same girl. Finally, in a fearless act of self-sacrifice as the bush fire closed on them, Bannerman traded his faster bay mare for his friend's slow grey. The hero was swallowed by the flames.

To help things along, Mr. Whitson spent the last half hour of a languid Friday afternoon reciting the thing with dramatic flourish to the whole classroom. *I rode through the Bush in the burning noon / Over the hills to my bride / The track was rough and the way was long. / And Bannerman of the Dandenong, / He rode along by my side. The teacher's voice rose and fell but was too high pitched to capture the drama of the galloping horses.*

For the very last verse he lowered his voice almost in prayer, *We dwell in peace, my beautiful one and I, / by the streams in the West, / - But oft through the mist of my dreams along, / Rides Bannerman of the Dandenong, / With the blood red rose on his breast.*

The senior class was to take turns reciting verses at random on Monday.

"I expect everyone to know it," he said with a threatening tone before dismissing class.

Everybody remembered what they did and didn't do on the weekend in question simply because of the momentous events that came later. The movie boat came on Friday and Gid, the movie man from across the bay, showed "The Law Comes to Texas" starring Hopalong Cassidy, to a packed house.

All next day the boys re-enacted the movie, bringing the law to Jossie's Meadow. They came well-armed, some with their carved wooden six shooters, others with silver cap pistols and gun belts from last Christmas. Still others brought lariats in case they needed to rustle domestic livestock. A band of evil bandits better known as the Gooseberry Gang quickly came together. With mud smeared faces they galloped off in the direction of a nearby grove of woods to lay in ambush for Freddie and Howie who this day wanted to be the Lone Ranger and Tonto.

Along the way, the outlaws raided Aunt Polly's vegetable garden and stuffed their pockets with plump green peas and sweet yellow carrots, making sure they took enough for the Lone Ranger and his sidekick as well. And all this without a thought for Bannerman although it crossed Freddie's mind that they ought to catch fire to the dry grass and re-enact that story too.

On Saturday night they were all too tired to memorize the long poem. On Sunday they had to attend morning service followed by sunday school at the church. Mr. Whitson's straight backed presence in the front row at eventide service was a harsh reminder that tomorrow was not far off. The hour of worship drew to a close with Rev. Snow leading the congregation in a rendition of the old Methodist hymn "The Shining Light." The boys and girls lifted their voices in song: *When I review my ways, / I dread impending doom. / But sure a friendly whisper says, / "Flee from the wrath to come." / My former hopes are fled. / My terror now begins. / I feel alas! That I am dead / In trespasses and sins…*

Next morning at precisely 9 AM on the ticking alarm clock Mr. Whitson led an enthusiastic rendition of "God Save the Queen" and classes resumed for the week. The younger ones were assigned copying exercises. His attention was then directed to the senior class and the demonstration of their poetry memorization skills.

"Now class, I want each of you to take turns reciting a verse of this wonderful poem and I want you to stand beside your desk when I call your name," said Mr. Whitson, "Ruby, you can start."

"I rode through the bush…," intoned Ruby, standing straight, and in a clear voice rattled off the first verse much to the teacher's delight.

He interrupted Betsy's enthusiastic delivery of the second verse in her sing-songy voice to point out how the lines flowed together for meaning. Betsy repeated the lines and Mr. Whitson shifted his attention across the room to the boys.

"Now, Freddie, The third verse." There was an uneasy silence.

"I don't know it, sir," said Freddie blankly.

"What was the song he sang that day?" inquired Mr. Whitson, trying to provide a cue to Freddie's brain.

"I don't know, sir," replied Freddie again.

"Red, red rose of the Western streams, was the song he sang that day," interrupted Ruby, in an effort to deflect attention from Freddie. "Bay Mathinna, his peerless steed…" Ruby would have continued but was cut short by the teacher.

"That's enough, Ruby. I want this lazy lout to answer." He was now standing in front of Freddie with his strap in hand. "Perhaps you would care to explain why you did not do your homework, Mr. Freddie," said the teacher sarcastically.

"I was riding through the bush, sir, in the burning noon."

A nervous giggle began spreading around the room and was only halted by the angry glare of the teacher. To emphasize the point he brought the strap across Freddie's behind. Then Freddie stiffened and turned to face the teacher.

"You're not to hit me again, sir. My mother said so."

"Is that so, Frederick?" The teacher's angry voice rose. "You are to go and stand by my desk until the lesson is finished, then we'll see how that strip of leather will change your attitude." Freddie walked obediently to the desk. It was obvious that the confrontation was only delayed.

The teacher's attention shifted to the next student. "There fell a spark on the upland grass," Mr. Whitson recited. "Now, Howie, What happens next?"

"I don't know sir," said Howie with a blank look.

"And what is your excuse, Mr. Howie," inquired Mr. Whitson, as he realized his lesson was falling apart.

Howie looked towards Freddie standing by the teacher's desk. "I was riding, too, sir, with Bannerman of the Dandenong."

This time the giggles had turned to involuntary bursts of laughter across the classroom. A fleeting cloud of uncertainty crossed the teacher's face.

Mr. Whitson strode purposely back to his desk and summoned Howie to come forward as well. A hush settled over the room. The show of insolence, he realized, was a challenge to his supreme authority. If left unpunished it would lead to a breakdown of order.

These two would be an example to the rest. He was now shaking with intense anger and drew in his breath sharply to control his quavering voice as he hissed at the boys. "Mr. Freddie, if you will not do as you are told in this school, I will take it out of your hide. Now, hold out your hands," he commanded.

Mr. Whitson seized the brown leather strap and raised it above his shoulder rocking back on his heels as he did so to obtain maximum force. The deadly instrument of pain arched through the air towards the outstretched palm.

Then the unexpected happened. Freddie withdrew his hand at the last split second and the strap snapped against the teacher's thigh. As Mr. Whitson winced in pain Freddie's calm voice filled the room.

"We will take no more straps in this school, sir."

And with that the two boys turned and walked from the room. The loud ticking of the alarm clock heightened the silence of the classroom and a house fly, awakened too soon from its autumn slumber, buzzed furiously against the window pane.

Rue came and talked to the teacher next morning during recess. No one knew what was said but a regulation strap made of hard rubber and canvas, precisely sixteen inches long and one and one half inches wide, replaced the previous hand crafted strip of leather on Mr. Whitson's desk.

A change came over him after that. He spent long periods sitting in subdued silence at his desk, often not even bothering to assign work to his students. His clock, too, fell silent for want of winding.

Outside, the seasons changed, fall gave way to winter, and each day, just past mid-afternoon, daylight was chased away by gloomy darkness. One cold December morning, a week before Christmas, Mr. Whitson announced that he was resigning and would not return in the New Year.

January brought another teacher, Mr. Babcock, an overweight, jolly man and a free thinker. He surprised everyone on the first day during Geography class when he threw the globe into the closet and announced that the Island formed one of the four corners of a flat earth. Somehow the students found it a comforting thought.

THE STRANGLING ANGEL

We have no specific remedy for any of the acute ... diseases.
...The specific disease is not cut short - it is not cured by our
remedies; it runs its course, do what we may to prevent it.

Sir William Jenner,
Lectures and Essays on Fevers and Diphtheria
1849 to 1879

MARTHA Earle, was just 42 years of age in the winter of 1892 when the strangling angel was claiming the lives of the young and the old on the Island.

Martha had met her future husband, James, around 1875 when he was an unattached bachelor living in Twillingate. The historical records describe her as a spinster, without visible means and several years his senior, living at New Bay Head. They crossed paths and began planning a life together. There is no record of their romantic relationship but we can draw conclusions from subsequent events. In 1877 Martha was engaged as a household servant by Strong & Murcells, wealthy merchants in Little Bay Islands, some forty-five miles from Twillingate as the crow flies. In the age of small sailboats on the coast this was a rather challenging journey for continuing a courtship.

The following summer, a lovelorn James rowed and sailed his skiff across Notre Dame Bay from Kettle Cove, Twillingate Island, to Little Bay Islands. Along the way

We learn that diphtheria has been prevalent at Ward's Harbour of late and that a good many cases have proved fatal. We are sorry that Mr. Samuel Short has lost three children, from this disease.

Twillingate Sun, Oct. 25, 1891

he scouted promising locations for a home and a fishing enterprise. After making a decision he proposed to Martha.

She took leave of her employer, accompanied James to his dream harbour, and they set to work building a winter home at Island Cove on the western end of Long Island. When it was completed in October of 1878 they were married at the Strong house in a simple ceremony conducted by the Methodist clergyman on his fall circuit of Notre Dame Bay.

They were modest, uncomplicated people, and like most of their generation in the outport villages along the coast, neither could read or write but were determined to carve a livelihood from the sea and the land.

Island Cove was a cozy harbour, sheltered from the open sea, and offering just enough good soil to plant vegetable gardens. The hard working couple prospered by the standards of the time. The family grew with the births of four healthy boys, first Herb in 1879, Titus in 1882, Sim in 1883, and Wilson in 1884. James started a small lobster canning operation to complement his income from fishing in the summer. In winter he and the boys canned rabbits for Strong and Murcells. They were growing quickly into young men and everything possible had to be done to give them a good start.

Martha did not become pregnant again until August of 1891. James was hoping for another boy who would be named John in honour of his own father, who had been caught in a fierce fall storm, and had disappeared forever on a bird hunting trip in November of 1859. The sudden loss had devastated the family and had thrust the then ten year old James into a role as breadwinner for the family.

Things went well until January when Martha was confined to bed with fever and a severe sore throat, symptoms which eased somewhat as winter wore on. The mysterious illness, however, kept her in a fragile condition and unable to care for the family. James suspected the worst.

A silent killer was stalking the island at the time. It struck often in the dead of night, in the most unexpected places, and respected neither rich nor poor. The evil presence waited to inflict its sorrow in the dark days of late fall and early winter when children were weak and less well fed. It snatched mothers in childbirth as well as the newborn children, and crept silently on to the next unsuspecting home. Infants and young children were often gone in several days. Sometimes the suffering lasted several weeks.

For stronger adults the fight for survival could last much longer. Lethal poisons left behind in the body slowly destroyed the heart, the nerves, and even the eyes. The tell-tale mark of the disease was a dark leathery membrane in the shape of angel wings spread around the tonsils and over the windpipe of the dead.

IN THE POLICE COURTS before F. Berteau, Esq. On Monday last, Mr. George Rice, of Little Hr., charged with violation of the Public health Act, by allowing his family to go abroad, while his house was under quarantine for diphtheria: and also for removing the flag before the house was disinfected. He pleaded ignorance of the law, and was let off, by paying $3.15, being the costs. Also Mr. John Spencer, of same place on a similar charge, having gone to Church and other places from a house infected with diphtheria. He has to pay the costs, $2.99.

Twillingate Sun, March 28, 1896

No one understood where it came from or how it reached the island. Everyone blamed sailors from foreign parts who landed at St. John's or Twillingate, without proper quarantine. They had hidden the fact of the grim reaper's presence on their ships.

The schooners from the island had come back from their annual supply run to St. John's in October with stories of hundreds of deaths in the city and thousands more, sick.

The government in St. John's had made a law to stop the strangling angel. On pain of imprisonment not exceeding three months or a fine not exceeding $100 everyone would have to report its presence to a justice of the peace or a magistrate. No one from the afflicted homes would be allowed in a public place where it could be passed on to others.

The family in Island Cove felt safer than others on the Island. They were nearly half a mile from the main community and made only rare visits as necessary to trade and help friends.

James and Martha were close to John and Selena Parsons, both families having children of the same age. It was with shock and disbelief that James noticed the quarantine flag flying over his friend's home in late November.

All three of the Parsons' youngest children woke on the cold November morning in the fall of 1890 with a sore throat and a raging fever, finding it painful to laugh, and having trouble swallowing. By nightfall a dark membrane was starting to cover their tonsils, closing off their throat. Breathing was fast and croupy. The baby's neck was heavily swollen.

Selena put all three children together in one bed in the small upstairs room and opened the window hoping against hope that her babies would be spared, hoping that whatever had her children in its grasp would fly away, that the fresh air would cleanse the house. And, everyone knew that someone across the bay had done the same thing and the children had gotten better. She refused to allow her husband and the older children up the stairs for fear they would be next.

She asked John to row across the bay to Strong's store to get Minard's Linament, because it was the only medicine she could think of. The children died within a few days of each other and were buried in a common grave, Lily, 4 years old, Herbert, only two, and John, the baby, just three short months.

A CURE FOR DIPHTHERIA
The following remedy was discovered in Germany and is said to be the best known: At the first indication of diphtheria in the throat of the child make the room close; then take a tin cup and pour into it a quantity of tar and turpentine, equal parts. Then hold the cup over a fire so as to fill the room with fumes, the person affected will cough up and spit out all the membraneous matter; and the diphtheria will pass off. The fumes of the tar and turpentine loosen the matter in the throat and thus affords the relief that has baffled the skill of physicians.

Twilingate Sun, Jan. 25, 1890

Everyone recognized they were helpless against the killer. It was in the air and under the ground and even blew in on the cold northeast wind whistling around the window panes in the dead of night.

James had walked the short distance on the sea ice from Island Cove to Lush's Bight to try and make it easier for his friend's family to cope with their loss. He scraped a single grave from the frozen earth in the Methodist Cemetery and helped with the simple burial.

Perhaps this was when he had brought the thing back to his own place. It lay lurking under the boughs on the dirt floor waiting for a helpless child to walk by. Perhaps he should have stayed home because half the houses had warning flags flying in the breeze. And hadn't Tommy Brooks, the lay-minister, told him he had buried over twenty children on the island in the past few years.

It was either God's will or the devil's punishment.

Throughout February and early March, Martha was still confined to bed, eating little, but for the time being not getting noticeably weaker. Mrs. Brookes, the midwife, came for a few days giving James a break. She passed along her own alarming diagnosis that the expectant mother was probably still suffering from a sinister form of diphtheria which must now be attacking her heart. She had witnessed it before. The unborn child was still moving but there wasn't much hope that either the mother or a newborn would come through. With the strangling angel in the home, James had a critical decision to make.

Even with the four boys isolated in the other bedroom of the rough tilt, he was convinced that sooner or later, the disease would strike them. He would have to find a safe shelter for them somewhere on the island.

At the end of March, with Martha still in a weakened condition and unable to get out of bed James took the boys by dog team down the winter trail to Edward Slade's home. They struck a bargain that the boys would stay with the Slade family until the baby was born and Martha recovered. The boys, all healthy and strong would help out in Edward's gardens and in his fishing business as if they were part of his own family. It was to be a beneficial arrangement for both families.

In early April as long sunny days were beginning to brighten the island, Martha went into labour and the baby, a boy, as James had wished for, was born. The father's happiness with his new son was short lived as the mother quickly weakened further under the stress of childbirth. On the morning of the 6th of April, 1892 the mid-wife emerged from the bedroom to announce that Martha had passed away. The frail baby too appeared to be gravely ill.

A grief stricken James took Martha's body by dog team on its last journey down the snow covered trail to the cemetery. The lay minister conducted a short funeral service and then accompanied James back to Island Cove to baptize the struggling child, John Colbourne, the fifth son of James and Martha.

On April 15, 1892, nine days after his mother died John was taken by the strangling angel.

THE epidemic continued unabated on the island until 1898. Records indicate that as many as one hundred residents succumbed to the disease in the ten years period dating from 1888. In many cases where burials were conducted by grieving parents or by lay ministers there is no record. More than eighty percent of those who died were infants and young children.

THE GOOSE OF CHRISTMAS PAST

*There never was such a goose. Bob said he didn't believe
there ever was such a goose cooked. Its tenderness and flavour, size and cheapness were the themes of universal ad-
miration. Eked out by the apple sauce and mashed potatoes, it was a sufficient dinner for the whole family..., and
the youngest Cratchits in particular were steeped in sage
and onion to the eyebrows!*

Charles Dickens, A Christmas Carol

ON Thursday night we had been allowed to stay up late.
Mother wanted us to hear the big announcement from Ot-
tawa on our grandmother's radio. The next day, a bright
Spring Friday at the beginning of April, 1949, nearly everyone on our little Island was celebrating confederation
with Canada.

Canadian and Newfoundland flags flew side by side
in the light breeze. The flags looked all the same to us
because there was a lot of red. The Union Jack flew at
half-mast near one house with black curtains. A small parade led by reluctant Orangemen who preferred to march
on July 12th wound its way round the community with
school children waving small red pennants and dogs nip-
ping at their heels. The church bell rang. There was a
community feast, candy for the children and gunfire in
the evening.

A far more momentous event had occurred earlier in

the day in our uncle's barn. The first domestic goose any children on the island had ever seen was hatched. We had only watched the distant flocks of wild geese flying overhead on their fall migration. Our uncle Rube who lived next door and owned a general store, had received four goose eggs in early March from a business friend in the city. The oversized eggs were placed under one of his broody hens which dutifully sat on them for the better part of the month.

On April-Fool's day the toiling hen must have decided that enough was enough and chose to abandon the unnaturally large eggs and when uncle Rube went to check in the morning only one egg was showing any sign of life. Soon a small beak broke through one end. He watched eagerly as the gosling awkwardly emerged on oversized feet, grabbed his outstretched finger in its beak and looked him squarely in the face.

The creamy bundle of fluff was brought into my uncle's house in a straw filled box. Its every need was attended to and henceforth the two became inseparable. As it became more active and confident in the weeks ahead, it sat on his lap when called and ate chicken feed from his hand. Within a month it had outgrown its box in the porch and had become nearly as big as the hens, its new companions in the barn. The relationship was not pleasant since the space was small and the resident rooster resented the intruder in the flock.

By the end of May the young goose was allowed to spend its days and nights outside in the garden grazing on the new shoots of grass and weeds as they emerged from the ground. The chickens too spent their days outside but showed no inclination to accept the stranger in their midst. Soon the growing bird asserted his claim to the entire barnyard, confining the lesser fowl to just a small corner.

A loud series of honks early each morning was a signal for Uncle Rube to bring food. If he was late in doing so the goose mounted the deck and loudly tapped its yellow beak against the porch door. After a substantial breakfast of oats and corn it followed him to his general store and waited patiently outside the entrance. At other times it was his companion when he tended his vegetable gardens across the big brook while the goose feasted on chickweed growing amongst the tender lettuce and cabbage plants.

It soon became obvious by its proud demeanor and bright blue eyes that the goose was in fact a gander and uncle Rube christened it Sir Gordon because according to him it bore an amazing resemblance to the departing British Governor, Sir Gordon Macdonald, who a few weeks earlier had aired his goodbyes to the good people of the island on the Broadcasting Corporation of Newfoundland.

"Canada will not be the goose that lays the golden eggs," He had said, "but life will certainly get better."

Fortunately for the nervous chickens, Sir Gordon began to spend more time investigating the wide stream running through the gardens, searching the steadies for succulent water plants. Often he allowed himself to be swept along by the current out to the sheltered harbour. There he kept a wary eye on approaching rowboats and suspicious looking children playing along the shoreline. At times the goose ran over the calm water flapping its wings as it tried to take flight.

By September Sir Gordon had established a predictable routine of searching for food to satisfy a ravenous appetite and keeping watch over his domain. He was no longer allowed to follow Uncle Rube and stand outside the general store because it was bad for business. When customers arrived they were confronted by a hissing gander with flapping wings, a frightening spectacle which put to flight even the most stout-hearted shoppers. After each incident Sir Gordon was banished back to the barnyard and soon learned to forgo the pleasure of walking to the general store each morning.

The vigilant goose, which could spot strangers a mile away, presented another set of problems for the many visitors to the busy household. The Reverend Snow, who regularly ministered to his flock in the community for the first week of each month, stayed at Uncle Rube's comfortable home during his clerical stopovers. On this first Saturday of September he was contemplating a warm cup of tea in his favourite easy chair as he strolled up to the gateway, humming the chorus from his favourite hymn.

He said later that he thought he was being attacked by the evil serpent himself as the goose began hissing and striking the calves of his legs with its open beak. The latch on the gate had clicked shut behind him and in dire panic he realized there was no escape as Sir Gordon mounted a full scale assault. The Reverend ran full flight for the deck and the open porch door with the attacker tight on his heels. As Sir Gordon flapped his wings in victory Reverend Snow collapsed in the kitchen and was administered a small glass of beef iron wine to calm his shattered nerves.

Uncle Rube took a week to contemplate the future of Sir Gordon; a choice between an early holiday feast and finding a new owner. In the end, because of the bond between the two, he realized he would never be able to eat a bird that had become a loyal pet and a misguided guardian of his property.

On a quiet evening in mid-September Uncle Rube led the bird into our barnyard to get it used to its new home. He announced to Father that the goose was now his and he should fatten it up for the family Christmas dinner.

It was a welcome gift in our household. Father had only just returned from the Labrador fishery and low prices for salt cod along with a poor catch had left him nearly penniless. The only bright spot was mother's family allowance cheque which was now coming from the Canadian government and would at least provide for flour, sugar, Good Luck Margarine and the occasional can of Horsey orange juice.

Sir Gordon now became the centre of attention around our home. From the beginning we began to visualize ourselves sitting around the dinner table with the succulent roasted goose as the centerpiece. We dreamed about the sizzling bird turning a golden brown in the oven with the savoury aromas wafting through the house. My older brothers argued over who would get the wish bone while my sister and I laid claim to the liver. Mother did not participate in the fantasy banquet, preferring instead to concentrate on the immediate challenge of putting daily food on the table.

Father had never raised a goose. He simply took the advice of his brother that he allow it outside as before to graze at will on the grass and weeds in the gardens and to swim in the nearby brook. It continued to forage around the harbour eating whatever it could find buried in the kelp on the shoreline. Sir Gordon became proficient at searching out juicy mussels amongst the seaweed and plump clams which he teased out of their hiding places in the sand with his beak. He learned to toss them against a rock with a flick of his outstretched neck to break the shells and uncover the sweet meat inside.

The children watched over the bird from a respectful distance, constantly refining their vision of the coming feast; the satiny dark gravy covering mashed potatoes; the fruity dressing flavoured by grandmother's fresh rosemary and sage; the crispy skin oozing golden oil over their taste buds.

Mother had certainly never cooked a goose and had never imagined in her wildest dreams being in the fortunate position of having such a majestic bird for Christmas. But as October passed into November even she could barely hide her excitement. Mother's friends dropped by, envious of our good fortune, offering cooking advice and subtly suggesting they might be offered a morsel of leftover on Boxing Day.

Grandmother Bessie visited often, expounding on the fact that the Royal Monarch himself preferred a roast goose for the great feast day in December. The best part, she'd say, would be the precious fat which would have to be skimmed off during cooking and carefully stored in mason jars to nourish the young ones in the cold winter months.

"Sliced bread soaked in beaten eggs and fried in goose fat will fortify the weakest constitution." she advised. "and there does not exist amongst mortal man a more glorious treat than sliced potatoes seared in the flavourful grease."

November turned out to be Indian summer that year and even the bright fall colours of the forest persisted with the unusually mild weather. Father set his nets to catch some of the giant Atlantic salmon which ran in late fall on their way back to the big rivers. The warm days also allowed Sir Gordon to carry on with his daily routine. He continued to visit his favourite feeding places along the beaches. In late evening he returned to the barnyard to receive his daily ration of chicken feed mixed with boiled salmon, which father was using to fatten him further for Christmas. He always left early in the morning, waking us with his loud honking before taking flight past our bedrooms windows on his short journey to the harbour.

The first cold spell came in early December as we were practicing our roles for the school Christmas concert. The highlight was to be a performance of *The Cratchits' Christmas Dinner* with my older brother as Bob Cratchit and myself as Tiny Tim due to my being the youngest and scrawniest in the school. 'And may God bless us everyone', was Tiny Tim's only line in the drama set around the Christmas table on the stage. Reality was soon to imitate art. We delivered our lines with great enthusiasm knowing that a real goose was soon to grace our family table.

Small crusty ice pans began to form on the sheltered harbour, a signal that complete freeze up and months long isolation from the mainland was not far off. The ice edge extended further and further out each day as the frosty weather continued. Fishermen hastened to pull all their boats up on the shore.

Father decided at this point to put Sir Gordon in the barn for fear he would be trapped in the ice or fall prey to a hungry fox. The barn door was open and the stall was ready when the goose returned for his late evening meal. As father, with outstretched arms, tried herding him towards the doorway, Sir Gordon extended his neck, hissed a warning and charged. Father sensibly retreated and the bird took wing back to the safety of the harbour.

Perhaps sensing a threat to his well- being, Sir Gordon did not return to our barnyard the next day or in the weeks ahead. For several days father discussed the situation with his friends and received many suggestions about how best to secure the fat goose in time for Christmas dinner.

Uncle Pliny, a crack shot, offered to come by with his lever action 44-40 rifle and dispatch the bird from a distance. Father said he didn't need a cannon.

Finally in desperation a day before Christmas Eve,

father and his younger brother decided to take the old three-quarter muzzle loader with them and launch a small rowboat over the ice out to the open water at the harbour mouth. His young brother thought that with a few extra fingers of gun powder in the musket it was a sure thing. Sir Gordon, though, had strengthened his position and kept a watchful eye on any movement along the shoreline.

Father realized when they had gone only a hundred yards that the expedition was hopeless as the goose demonstrated an uncanny ability to keep a constant distance between himself and the small boat by swimming towards the open sea. Sir Gordon turned and honked aggressively as if mocking the two hunters as they returned to shore in defeat dragging their small boat with them.

Christmas Eve arrived with newly fallen snow. All the children were excited about receiving gifts from Santa Claus at the village Christmas concert in the evening. At our house there was a gloom which could not be dispelled even by the small decorated tree in the corner and the gingery smell of baking cookies.

We saw no sign of Sir Gordon in the open water at the harbour mouth during the day. Despite a thorough search not even a feather could be found and the dark reality dawned on us that we would not eat goose on Christmas Day. Father, with a deep sigh, suggested that Sir Gordon might have been swallowed by a passing shark.

Grandmother and Grandfather came by on their decorated sled pulled by Bob, their old Newfoundland pony. They had tied Christmas bells on his harness to lift our spirits. Grandmother gave us peppermint candy. She observed that Sir Gordon must have been yearning for the southlands and had hooked up with a late migrating flock of Canada Geese.

During the performance of *The Cratchit's Christmas Dinner*, Tiny Tim contemplated the dry paper mache goose in the centre of the table and burst into tears. Mr. Cratchit had to deliver his line.

BIBLIOGRAPHY

DeMont, John. *Coal Black Heart*. Anchor Canada, 2009.

Fox, Colin. *Monchy Le Preux*. Pen and Sword Books Ltd., Barnsley, UK. 2000.

Gallishaw, John. *Trenching at Gallipoli: The Personal Narrative of a Newfoundlander with the Ill Fated Dardenelles Expedition*. New York: The Century Company, 1917.

Imperial War Museum. *The Diary of the Royal Newfoundland Regiment*.

Keegan, John. *The First World War*. Vintage Canada. 2000.

Lind, Francis T. *The Letters of Mayo Lind*. St. John's: Killick Press, 2001

Nicholls, Jonathan. *Cheerful Sacrifice: The Battle of Arras 1917*. Pen and Sword Books Limited, Barnsley, UK. 2003.

Nicholson, G. W. L. *The Fighting Newfoundlander: A History of the Royal Newfoundland Regiment*, Second Edition. Montreal & Kingston: Mcgill-Queens University Press, 2006.

Smallwood, J. R. *Book of Newfoundland,* Vol. 1. Edited by Joseph R. Smallwood, St. John's: Newfoundland Book Publishers, 1937.

Records of the First World War. Used with the permission of the Provincial Archives of Newfoundland and Labrador.

Stacy, Anthony. J. and Jean Edwards Stacy, *Memoirs of a Blue Puttee: The Newfoundland Regiment In World War One*. St. John's: DRC Publishers, 2002.

The Twillingate Sun. Excerpts used with the permission of Memorial University Archives.

ACKNOWLEDGMENTS

The sources of information are too many to cite, but I want to mention a few of them. My first thanks go to Job Burton, a well-known elder of Long Island who has a memory like no other. Whenever I needed a piece of information I went to see Job. I must also thank Hedley Morgan for telling me the interesting stories about his grandfather.

My appreciation is extended to the staff of the Rooms Provincial Archives of Newfoundland and Labrador (PANL). They were indispensable in guiding me to the right places. The Imperial War Museum in London, England provided a copy of the War Diary of the Royal Newfoundland Regiment. Memorial University of Newfoundland provided access to the historical editions of the Twillingate Sun through their digital archives initiative.

The Children of the Beatrix Potter School in South London, England, deserve special recognition for their dedication in documenting the lives of Newfoundland soldiers buried at Wandsworth Cemetery. They located the grave of Private Heath and sent me a photo of the headstone.

And to my wife, Marilyn who was the editor and kept after me to get it finished.

ABOUT THE AUTHOR

Eric Colbourne was born at Lush's Bight, Long Island, NL in 1944. After completing high school he attended a six week summer school program designed to prepare 'emergency supply' teachers for remote communities in Newfoundland and Labrador. His first teaching post was at Ship Cove on the Great Northern Peninsula. He was  15 years old. He taught for three more years before going on to complete a B.A. and a B. Ed. from Memorial University. In 1974-75 he attended the University of Reading in England where he received a Diploma in Environmental Studies. He completed a M.A. at McGill University in 1987.

Most of his career was spent in Nunavut and the Northwest Territories where he served as a teacher, principal, school board director, and senior level administrator with the Department of Education, Culture and Employment.

Eric retired in 1998 and for ten years operated a B&B, with his wife, Marilyn, in a pastoral setting overlooking the ocean in Heart's Delight, NL. They have three grown children and four grandchildren.

He has come full circle and once again resides in Lush's Bight, his birthplace.

CPSIA information can be obtained
at www.ICGtesting.com
Printed in the USA
LVOW12s2305061217
558942LV00001B/7/P